Art Connections

Integrating Art Throughout the Curriculum

Kimberly Boehler Thompson
Diana Standing Loftus

Illustrations by
Kathleen Bullock and
Kimberly Boehler Thompson

GoodYearBooks

An Imprint of ScottForesman
A Division of HarperCollinsPublishers

Cover illustrations:

Pablo Picasso. *Guitar.* Céret (after March 31, 1913). Pasted paper, charcoal, ink and chalk on blue paper mounted on ragboard, 26 1/8 x 19 1/2". The Museum of Modern Art, New York. Nelson A. Rockefeller Bequest. Photograph © 1994 The Museum of Modern Art, New York.

Cover illustration excerpted from *Experiments in Optical Illusion* by Nelson F. Beeler and Franklyn M. Branley. Illustrated by Fred H. Lyon. Copyright 1951 by Thomas Y. Crowell. Reprinted by permission of HarperCollins Publishers, Inc.

GoodYearBooks

are available for most basic curriculum subjects plus many enrichment areas. For more GoodYearBooks, contact your local bookseller or educational dealer. For a complete catalog with information about other GoodYearBooks, please write:

GoodYearBooks
ScottForesman
1900 East Lake Avenue
Glenview, IL 60025

Book design by Amy O'Brien Krupp.
Copyright © 1995 Kimberly Boehler Thompson and Diana Standing Loftus.
All Rights Reserved.
Printed in the United States of America.

ISBN 0-673-36080-6

8 9 - MH - 02 01 00 99 98

Contents

From *Art Connections*, published by GoodYearBooks. Copyright © 1995 Kimberly Boehler Thompson and Diana Standing Loftus.

Introduction

Educators recognize art as an integral part of a well-rounded education. Although the wording in state goals may differ, the components of art education are consistent. They include:

Art Production

Art production refers to the art-making process. This component is what most people think of as "classroom art." The component should include knowledge of and experience with materials, tools, and techniques. From this foundation, students develop skills that allow for enriched self-expression.

Art History or Art Heritage

This component leads to an understanding of how art records and reflects various cultures. Students learn to question the who, what, when, where, and why of an art piece. This results in the ability to recognize and appreciate artworks from cultures past and present.

Art Criticism

Art criticism teaches students to recognize the elements and principles of design and the technical and expressive qualities of art. Through the Art Criticism component, students learn how to interpret art content and meaning, which enables them to discuss works of art using appropriate vocabulary.

Aesthetic Understanding

This component analyzes characteristics that classify an object as art. Students learn to identify factors that influence the meaning of an art object. Aesthetic understanding combines the abilities to see, interpret, evaluate, and express individual understanding.

Different components can be used to plan goal-oriented art experiences. Every lesson will not include all components. Whenever possible, however, planning an art lesson should include consideration of the components that will support the art process.

Purpose

Art Connections has been designed with three ideas in mind. The first is to provide elementary teachers with a resource that will build on their understanding of art. The second is to provide students with meaningful art experiences that use a variety of materials and techniques. The third is to suggest ways to integrate art into the curriculum.

How to Use This Book

The first five lessons of Art Connections introduce basic concepts. These lessons address components that create a foundation for the activities found in the book.

Two of these lessons, Art Talk and Looking for Meaning, approach fundamental art issues without requiring any art production. Instead, the lessons are models for leading research, discussions, and games that illustrate the issues.

Elements and Principles of Design and Color Studies each include a project that applies the concept introduced in the lesson. These concepts should be considered basic to any art production experience that includes making choices about shape, line, texture, space, or color, and the arrangement of these elements.

Evaluation Is an Inside Job is a crucial element in this book. The ideas in this section introduce creative problem solving and help guide self-evaluation. Students are encouraged to view their work in a positive, more objective way, enabling them to find meaning in any perceived imperfection.

Following these five opening sections are fourteen lessons within the production component. These lessons develop knowledge of art processes and skills using a variety of materials, tools, and techniques. Each lesson contains information that will support historical inquiry through discussion or research. These lessons follow a consistent format and were designed for integration with objectives from other subject areas. At the beginning of each lesson is a quote and a brief introduction. This is followed by a little history on the lesson topic, procedures to be used for the project, ideas to be integrated, a suggested list of resource books for students, teachers, and parents, and an occasional reproducible page.

Each of the fourteen lessons has two titles. The first title refers to the art concept; the second refers to the topic that is being integrated. Applications of the topics can be found under the Integrating Ideas section of the lesson. Suggestions are made for enhancing a unit of study. The book lists are for support for further exploration.

Integration

> Two stonecutters were engaged in similar activity. Asked what they were doing, one answered, *"I'm squaring up this block of stone."* The other replied, *"I'm building a cathedral."*
>
> *Willis Harman,* Global Mind Change, *1988*

This quote can be used to express the idea of integration; that is, seeing the whole picture rather than each part separately. *Art Connections* provides a springboard for integrating art with other subjects. It includes activities that deal with higher-level thinking skills and real-life experiences. This framework provides opportunities for children to question and make their own connections. Integrating becomes a way of thinking, a way of looking at our world, a tapestry in which the various threads are woven and interrelated to create a whole, pleasing image.

Extensions

It may be helpful to use an interest survey at the beginning of the year to learn about your students' past art experiences. The information from this survey can help in planning future art experiences. The same survey can be given at the end of the year as a follow-up. Suggested questions are included in a reproducible page at the end of this section.

Acknowledgements

Many family members and friends have encouraged, inspired, edited, and cheered. Special thanks in particular to our sons Justin Loftus and Ted Thompson, parents Viola and Walter Boehler and Maria Bezerra, Tom Thompson, Bill Kirkman, Sherry Joiner, Geni Moots, Sheila Drescher, Melissa Katsikis, Ken Loftus, Bill Mayer, Ted Loftus, and Tim Julian. Thanks also to those who have added to our knowledge: our editors Roberta Dempsey and Camille Salerno, Richard LaTour, Carol Howser, Kathleen Bullock, Donna Cooper, Karen Dalrymple, Carol McKay, Pam Sessions, Dona Zimmerman, and Mary Cooper. Finally, we're sincerely grateful to our students, particularly David Bish and Ester Devine, for perspectives gained from their art journals. It is from children that we gain new insights into our teaching and into ourselves.

Art Survey

1. What is art?

2. How do you feel about art?

3. Tell about your most exciting art experience.

4. Tell about your most frustrating art experience.

5. What are your favorite kinds of art activities?

6. Do you feel art is an important subject? Why or why not?

7. Who is your favorite artist?

8. In what areas of art would you like to know more?

PEANUTS reprinted by permission of UFS, Inc.

Art Talk

Investigating Children's Books

Learning to Talk About Art

One vital component in art education is art criticism. These two words are enough to raise any teacher's level of insecurity, not to mention his or her protective instincts for his or her students. The term is misleading; consequently, many educators refer to this realm as "talk about art." This lesson uses illustrated children's books as an exciting visual resource. The end-of-the-lesson project will apply the questions asked in this lesson to a discussion of a selected illustration. Students will respond with words and a drawing.

When a person responds to a piece of art, he or she is, in a sense, entering into a conversation. When an object "speaks," everyone will hear something slightly different. This is because a person's response is influenced by who he or she is, his or her mood, and his or her background. Naturally, those who are familiar with the language of the visual arts will have a better understanding of what's being said.

During a visual conversation, a person can ask three questions that will lead to greater understanding and appreciation of the artwork: 1. Who is the artist? 2. What is the work trying to communicate? 3. How is the idea or mood being expressed? Other sections of this book, such as Looking for Meaning pp. 16-25; Elements and Principles of Design pp. 26-33; and Color Studies pp. 34-43, will add to this visual vocabulary and help develop skills of observation and evaluation.

Use the information in this lesson as a guide to talk about art. Look at children's books, art books and, if possible, visit an art gallery or museum.

Who Is the Artist?

At the root of every work of art is the artist. The elements of expression chosen by an individual reflect something of that person—personality, mood, skill, heritage, and place in time. While it's certainly possible to appreciate artwork without the artist's biography, the communication may be more satisfactory if you're at least introduced.

A little detective work on an artist's life helps the viewer become aware of the artist's style, the way his or her style developed, and the influences that contributed to it. Information on well-known artists can be found in books on art history, museum books, and magazines such as *Art News*.

Students studying illustrators and authors can use the *Horn Book* magazine to learn about artists who have received the Caldecott Honor for children's books. For example, investigate the works of author and illustrator Chris Van Allsburg. Compare the pictures from his first book, *The Garden of Abdul Gasazi,* with his later work. How are the illustrations similar, how are they different? What words can be used to describe his style? Look for distinctive qualities such as the signature bull terrier that repeatedly appears in Van Allsburg's books. Think about his background as a sculptor. Does this show in his drawings? Research artists that Van Allsburg admires, including Balthûs, René Magritte, and Edward Hopper. Can you see evidence of their influence in his illustrations? Look for illustrations by Chris Van Allsburg that reveal a style similar to Magritte's *Time Transfixed,* shown here. Has Chris Van Allsburg influenced others? Look for the book *BaBa,* written and illustrated by Tanya Shpakow, a student of Chris Van Allsburg. This lovely book is an example of how one artist's work can be distinctively different yet still show the imprint of another artist.

René Magritte, Belgian, 1898–1967. *Time Transfixed,* oil on canvas, 1938, 146.1 x 97.5 cm, Joseph Winterbotham Collection, 1970.426, photograph courtesy of The Art Institute of Chicago.

What Is the Work Trying to Communicate?

What is the idea behind a work of art? What is the artist's intention? The answers to these questions will help bring us closer to discovering why the work was created—be it to express a mood, an idea, or an ideal.

It is usually easy to recognize the idea behind a book illustration. The paintings of Beatrix Potter are visually communicating the story as she sees it. We expect story illustrations to interpret the text. How is the artist doing this? Is the work literal and very realistic, or does the artist seem to be more interested in expressing the mood of the story?

It can be more difficult to understand the artist's intention when looking at work in a museum or art gallery. The artist may choose to simply represent a subject or tell a story. More often, however, the meaning of the work goes beyond the subject.

The Subject of a Woman with Many Different Meanings

Louvre, Paris

Giraudon/Art Resource, NY

Arrangement in Grey and Black, 1872. James Whistler's interest in abstraction is reflected in the title of the painting, but the subject is his mother.

La Desserte rouge (Harmony in Red), 1908-09. Henri Matisse often uses a woman as his subject. In this painting, he is exploring pictorial space, mainly interested in line and color.

Willem de Kooning. *Woman, I.* (1950–52). Oil on canvas, 75 7/8 x 58'. The Museum of Modern Art, New York (Purchase).

Pablo Picasso. *Girl before a Mirror.* Boisgeloup (March 1932). Oil on canvas, 62 x 51 1/4'. The Museum of Modern Art, New York. Gift of Mrs. Simon Guggenheim.

Woman, I, 1950-52. Willem De Kooning's abstract expressionist painting only loosely suggests the form of a woman. De Kooning's interest was in the tension created in a work that combines abstract and figurative painting.

Girl before a Mirror, 1932. Pablo Picasso's subject is a young woman posed in contemplation in front of a mirror. He is interested in both the rhythmic color patterns of curvilinear cubism and in the mystery of the classical theme of woman.

When looking at a piece of art, contemplate why the artist may have created it. Process and technique can be important clues. The title of the artwork may also hint at the concept. Ask for information or read any materials that may accompany an art exhibit.

How Is the Idea Being Expressed?

The old expression "It's not what you say, but how you say it" can be applied to artistic communication. The form or subject of a piece of art has three qualities important to the idea behind it: its **sensory**, **technical**, and **expressive** properties. These properties influence the message of a piece of art and our response to it.

Sensory Properties

The sensory properties are also called the elements of design. These properties are line, shape, color, texture, and the positive and negative space. When talking about art, it's best to keep the discussion of these elements simple. Discuss each element. Describe the line. What could you say about the colors? the shapes? (See Elements and Principles of Design pp. 26-33.)

Technical Properties

The materials and techniques chosen by the artist help define the expressive characteristics of a work of art. When visiting an art gallery or museum, compare different line and surface qualities found in drawings (pencil, charcoal, pastel), paintings (oil, acrylic, watercolor), and original prints (etchings, woodcuts, silkscreen, or lithographic prints). Each process has a look and a feeling that is unique.

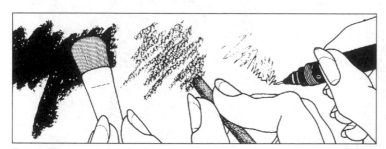 

Drawing

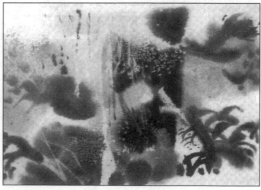

Watercolor

Etching

Woodcut

Expressive Properties

Sensory and technical properties often work together to express a feeling or idea. Notice the types of lines, colors, shapes, and surface textures used to develop different story illustrations. Think about how the artist's materials and techniques help convey the message. Expressive properties can be explored using a rich variety of children's books. Begin the adventure with a close look at the styles of Maurice Sendak *(Where the Wild Things Are, Everyone Knows What a Dragon Looks Like)* and John Steptoe *(Mufaro's Beautiful Daughters—An African Tale).*

Airbrush

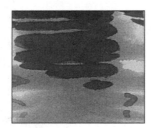

Wash

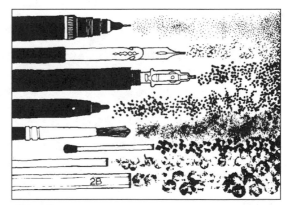

Stippling

Hatching

Crosshatching

> *"By appreciation, we make excellence in others our property."*
>
> *Voltaire*

Drawing from Illustrations

Drawing from existing art is a time-tested activity. For centuries apprentices have learned by emulating the masters. Then, as culture grew protective of individual expression, this exercise was used with some reserve. Today, art educators see the value of old practices. Like listening and speaking, drawing is a vehicle for learning. To copy or to interpret what another artist has done is another form of "knowing." The experience opens students' eyes to what is possible. Instead of limiting the individual, the experience contributes to a personal deposit of ideas and leads to richer forms of expression.

Materials

- drawing paper
- pencil
- colored pencils
- colored pens
- optional: water colors, tempera, brushes

Preparation

Find a stick to use as a pointer while talking about illustrations or works of art. Even a simple long and narrow dowel can entice students to get up and talk—and it makes them look eloquent. Discuss the ideas and questions already mentioned in the lesson. While talking, be sensitive to the energy of the group. Remember, the goal is to awaken interest.

Procedure

STEP 1.

When the class feels comfortable talking about art, pass out a list of questions and concepts similar to the ones already discussed in this lesson. Examples might include:

- What is the work trying to communicate?
- Do you think the artist's intention was to realistically illustrate the story or to express the mood? Explain.
- Discuss the sensory properties (line, shape, color, texture, positive or negative space)
- Discuss the technical properties. (How is the artwork made? What techniques are used?)
- If you were to give the work a title, what would it be?
- Talk about the artist if possible. Do you think the artwork reflects who that person is?

STEP 2.

As a group or individually, have students browse through books and select an illustration to examine using the questions.

STEP 3.

Have students respond to the questions by taking notes. Invite students to present their selected illustration. Allow them to use their notes. Presentations can be made in groups or to the entire class.

STEP 4.

Now have students draw the same illustration in one of the following ways:

- While looking at the picture, adding his or her own artistic influence
- From memory, adding his or her own artistic influence
- What happens next
- One student describes the picture again while another draws
- Draw the picture, change the mood
- Draw a different picture, but use the same sensory and technical properties

From *Art Connections*, published by GoodYearBooks. Copyright © 1995 Kimberly Boehler Thompson and Diana Standing Loftus.

Integrating Ideas

he following ideas encourage experiences that gain insight into authors and illustrators:

- Assemble a bulletin board which highlights a well-known artist, illustrator, or author. Have works from the highlighted artist available. Do this occasionally throughout the year, each time highlighting a different artist.

- An author's or illustrator's lifestyle, background, and interests can be reflected through children's books. For example, Byrd Baylor's love of the outdoors, life in the desert, and Native American influence are present in her stories. The experience of living in New York City is apparent in some of Ezra Jack Keats's books. *Watch Out for the Chicken Feet in Your Soup* shows the influence left by Tomie DePaola's Italian grandmother. Have students discover some of these influences on their own. When highlighting an author/illustrator, give students time to make their own observations and generalizations about that person. Then have students find background information on various authors and illustrators. (*Horn Book, Cricket,* and *Classmate* are good resources.) Also check the list at the end of this lesson titled "Books." Students may be pleasantly surprised by how close their observations are compared to the background information of an artist.

- Writers like Byrd Baylor have many illustrators. Discuss the differences in the artists styles. Note that her book *Animal Tracks* is illustrated with the use of photographs.

- Write a letter to an author or illustrator. Curiosity motivated one fifth-grade class to do this. They asked Chris Van Allsburg "Why are so many of your illustrations in black and white?" "Which comes first—your writing or your drawing?" "Tell us about the dog, Fritz, that appears (sometimes hidden) in all your books." It was very exciting to receive a reply.

- After students have a basic knowledge of various authors' styles of writing, arrange them into small groups. Give each group a stack of books written by the same author. Have students look at leads, topics, endings, imagery, humor, character development, adventure, point of view, and so forth. Have each group write a list of observations they've made of the author's style and share the list with the class.

- Compare illustrations in science and social studies texts to those in fiction books.

- Examine the following list of books that have won the Caldecott award over the past 10 years.

> 1992 *Tuesday.* David Wiesner. Clarion Books.
>
> 1991 *Black and White.* David Macaulay. Houghton Mifflin.
>
> 1990 *Lon Po Po.* Ed Young. Philomel.
>
> 1989 *Song and Dance Man.* Karen Ackerman. Knopf.
>
> 1988 *Owl Moon.* Jane Yolen. Philomel.
>
> 1987 *Hey, Al.* Arthur Yorinks. Farrar.
>
> 1986 *The Polar Express.* Chris Van Allsburg. Houghton Mifflin.

1985 *Saint George and the Dragon.* Retold by Margaret Hodges. Little Brown & Co.

1984 *The Glorious Flight.* Alice & Martin Provensen. Penguin U.S.A.

1983 *Shadow.* Marcia Brown. Macmillan.

1982 *Jumanji.* Chris Van Allsburg. Houghton Mifflin.

Invite students to give their opinion on why these books were chosen to receive this award.

Books

For Teachers and Parents

Book of Junior Authors & Illustrators, 6th ed.; edited by Sally Holmes Holtze. H. W. Wilson Co., 1989.

Chapman, Laura H. *Art: Images and Ideas.* Davis Publications, 1992.

Cromer, Jim. *Criticism, History, Theory and Practice of Art Criticism in Art Education.* The National Art Education Association, 1990.

Finn, David. *How to Visit a Museum.* Harry N. Abrams, Inc., 1985.

Greenberg, Jan, and Jordan, Sandra. *The Painter's Eye: Learning to Look at Contemporary American Art.* Delacorte Press, 1991.

McElmeel, Sharon L. *An Author a Month (for pennies).* Libraries Unlimited Inc., 1988.

Wilson, Brent; Hurwitz, Al; and Wilson, Marjorie. *Teaching Drawing from Art.* Davis Publications, 1992.

For Students

Bjork, Christina, and Anderson, Lena. *Linnea in Monet's Garden.* Raben & Sjogren Publishers. Stockholm, Sweden. 1985.

Brown, Laurene Krasny, and Brown, Marc. *Visiting the Art Museum.* E. P. Dutton, 1986.

Konigsburg, E.L. *The Second Mrs. Giaconda.* Aladdin Books, 1975.

Levy, Virginia K. *Let's Go to the Art Museum,* rev. ed. Harry N. Abrahms. 1988.

Reiner, Annie. *A Visit to the Art Galaxy.* Green Tiger Press, Inc., 1990.

Sullivan, Charles. *Imaginary Gardens, American Poetry and Art for Young People.* Harry N. Abrams, 1989.

Venezia, Mike. *Getting to Know the World's Greatest Artists.* Childrens Press, 1991. (Series includes: Da Vinci, Michelangelo, Botticelli, Rembrandt, Goya, Van Gogh, Gaugin, Monet, Paul Klee, Picasso, Hopper.)

Ventura, Piero. *Great Painters.* G.P. Putnam's Sons, 1984.

Yenawine, Philip. *Stories.* The Museum of Modern Art. Delacorte Press, 1991.

Looking for Meaning

Native American Legacies

Understanding Art and Culture

Ideally, the study of art in any culture begins with a willingness to suspend judgment. A person should seek to understand the beliefs, traditions, and everyday life of different cultures. Oftentimes, these beliefs, traditions, and lifestyles are reflected through art. Guidelines for describing and defining art are introduced in this lesson. These guidelines are used to examine and compare artwork objectively. The research outline and games at the end of the lesson can be used when learning about any culture. Using these, we can begin to understand the story art can tell.

When looking at the meaning of art historically, the idea of "art created for its own sake" is a new concept. Native American artworks, for example, were functional objects to be used by the people who made them (and eventually for trading purposes). "Special" objects were also made for religious or other ceremonial purposes. The symbols and patterns that adorned the objects often became tribal traditions that held specific meaning for

From *Art Connections*, published by GoodYearBooks. Copyright © 1995 Kimberly Boehler Thompson and Diana Standing Loftus.

that group of people. But common, everyday items were also decorated to make them more beautiful to look at.

Since the dawn of man, art has existed for different reasons: to give beauty to the form of a functional object; to give form to an idea or a feeling; to worship and to imitate nature; and to create patterns and compositions that delight our eyes. Art has taken us beyond our basic needs and given us an abundance of aesthetic opportunities.

Describing and Defining Art

What is art? This is an important question and there are many different ways of answering it. One way is to think about four qualities that may be used to describe art forms. 1) Art can imitate; it can represent any visible part of our world; 2) Art can be formal with an emphasis on design elements; 3) Sometimes art is expressive and 4) Sometimes it's functional. Any art object will have one or more of these qualities. Trying to describe and define art can stimulate observation and lead to an understanding of why the object was made (and why in this particular form).

"Is the piece of art I'm looking at imitational, formal, expressive, or functional?"

I M I T A T I O N A L :

Imitational art represents or imitates things in the real world. It may have been the intention of the artist to draw or paint nature as he or she saw it. Native American art forms were seldom imitational; this possibly being the result of limited materials and tools. Occasionally carved objects, paintings, and drawings made by Native Americans are found with qualities that belong in this category.

Smithsonian Institution National Anthropological Archives

FORMAL:

Formal art emphasizes elements and principles of design such as line, shape, balance, and rhythm. These elements and principles may take abstract or nonobjective forms. These qualities are found in most Native American art, from the beaded patterns of the plains and lakes people to the carved objects created by the forest and sea tribes.

EXPRESSIVE:

Expressive art has qualities that communicate a feeling or mood. This type of art may exaggerate reality rather than imitate it. Native American art is frequently expressive. The False Face masks of the Iroquois are very good examples.

FUNCTIONAL:

Functional art has a practical or religious function. This is the foundation of Native American art. Most examples will have this quality.

The objects and artistic traditions of Native American cultures are a legacy which tells the story of the people, who they were, and how they lived. There are many differences among the societies which first inhabited North America. The differences correspond with the influence of the physical environment and the social and religious customs of each group. The variety is reflected in their art forms. For example, many Native Americans were nomadic (tribes who changed residence with the season and secured food by hunting and gathering). The art of these people was limited to practical and portable items such as clothing, tools, or weapons with carved or painted decoration.

In areas where land and climate made it possible to grow adequate supplies of food, some groups eventually built more permanent communities. These farmers needed storage containers. This influenced their art. Baskets were woven from available materials. Pottery was made in the regions where clay deposits were found. Geometric patterns or free-form designs were painted or incised on the pottery before firing.

Some Native American groups became highly developed, stable societies. They prospered in environments that provided abundant resources for food and shelter. These individuals experienced more leisure time and became more specialized in their skills. The artworks that resulted were fine quality and often grand in scale; some were woven, others were carved from wood or stone.

Projects

Research and Response

Materials

- books on Native American art from school or public libraries
- examples of Native American artwork (pictures, postcards, posters)
- actual Native American objects (if possible)

Note: Materials collected should represent a broad range of art forms from various Native American cultures.

Procedure

STEP 1.

Talk about the qualities, examples, and terms already mentioned in the lesson.

STEP 2.

Divide the class into groups. Invite each group to appoint a researcher, a recorder, and a presenter. (All students of the group still participate in each task.)

S T E P 3 .

Let each group investigate the collected pictures and books on Native American art. Have them choose 5 examples to read about and/or observe. Then, using the following questions, have each group discuss each piece of art.

a) Who do you think made the object (man, woman, child)?

b) What was the purpose of the object?

c) Is the object decorated? Describe the object and the decoration (lines, shapes, colors, textures)

d) Why do you think it was decorated?

e) Is it art? Why or why not?

S T E P 4 .

Invite the group recorder to write down the facts about their chosen artworks and the group's responses to the questions. (By doing this, they are making a research/response report.) Remind students to use the correct terms to describe their chosen artworks. Is the work imitational? Does it have formal qualities? Is it expressive? Is it (was it) functional?

S T E P 5 .

Invite each group presenter to make an oral presentation of their research/response report, describing the qualities of each piece of art they have chosen.

Game

Your Vote Counts

 or this game, students will decide if various pieces of art contain realistic, formal, expressive, and/or functional qualities.

Materials

- pictures, postcards, or photocopies of Native American artworks
- index cards, tagboard, or paper plates

Procedure

STEP 1.

Have the class collect a variety of pictures, postcards, or photocopies of Native American art.

STEP 2.

Divide the class into groups of four. One student in each group is assigned the role of director; a second student is assigned the role of vote counter; a third student is assigned the role of recorder; and a fourth student is assigned the role of reporter.

STEP 3.

Have students make voting signs using index cards, tagboard, or paper plates. Each student needs four signs, one to represent each quality. The design on the sign should illustrate and name the concept.

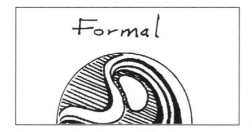

STEP 4.

Invite the class to look at the assortment of pictures, one at a time. Each student in each group should decide which quality or qualities the artwork contains and hold up the corresponding sign. (Remember, one object can have any or all of the qualities.)

From *Art Connections*, published by GoodYearBooks. Copyright © 1995 Kimberly Boehler Thompson and Diana Standing Loftus.

STEP 5.

The vote counter in each group records the results of the voting. The director gives everyone in his or her group two minutes to present and explain their point of view. (In the event of disagreement, emphasize that there are no wrong answers.) The group recorder takes notes mentioning comments, ideas, and observations of the group members. The group reporter delivers voting results and tells about his or her findings to the rest of the class.

Game

Art Market

roups of students select three artworks for their private art museum.

Materials

• at least 10 pictures of Native American art objects

Procedure

STEP 1.

Hang the pictures of Native American objects on a wall. Give each object a number.

STEP 2.

Divide the class into groups. Appoint one member of each group the committee chairperson, another member the recorder, a third member the treasurer, and a fourth member the group reporter.

STEP 3.

Ask each member of the group to write down the following phrases and fill in the blanks with the number of their chosen object.

◎ The one I like best   _____
◎ Most difficult to make   _____
◎ Most valuable   _____

◉ Most original   _____
◉ Best craftsmanship   _____
◉ Best design   _____
◉ The one I like least   _____
◉ The one I'd put in my house   _____

S T E P   4 .

Invite the treasurer in each group to collect the ballots. Ask the recorder to count the votes for each criteria.

S T E P   5 .

Have the committee chairperson from each group head a discussion to determine how his or her group will select their three works of art. For example, the group may choose to purchase objects from the highest votes in any category or they may limit the categories they would consider for their museum. Ask the group reporter to present voting results, selection process, and final choices to the class.

O P T I O N

To make things more exciting, let the groups compete in a silent auction, using votes to purchase artwork.

Integrating Ideas

◉ Questions that lead to understanding a culture can continue beyond art discussion and observation. After researching and responding to artwork, student groups can select a major Native American culture they wish to study in more depth. Listed below are names of tribes categorized by region.

Arctic and Subarctic: Eskimo, Kaska, Chippewa, Algonquin

Southwest: Pueblo, Navaho, Hopi, Zuni, Yuma, Apache

Northwest Coast: Coos, Chinook, Nootka, Haida, Tingit

Plains: Sioux, Crow, Cheyenne, Pawnee, Mandan, Blackfoot

California and Great Basin: Modoc, Shoshone, Ute, Pomo, Paiute, Nez Percé

Woodland: (Northeast) Iroquois, Delaware, Shawnee, Massachuset, Huron, Sauk, Narraganset; (Southeast) Cherokee, Creek, Seminole, Choctaw, Chickasaw

Instruct group members to take notes as they gather information about their chosen culture. Topics or questions to explore may include:

Tell about the art from the culture you chose.

Were any patterns, colors, or symbols frequently used? Explain.

What region is your Native American group from?

What seems to be important to them?

What are their customs?

How did the region influence the lifestyle of the people?

How do you think the region influenced the art?

Have students organize their notes into a presentation to give to the class. After group presentations, invite students to look for similarities and differences in the cultures (and art) of major Native American groups.

☻ Suggest students write about art from different points of view. For example, first have them imagine they are the artist; then have them imagine they are art historians or art critics.

☻ These ideas can be used to research art and culture in different parts of the world at different periods in history.

Books

For Teachers and Parents

Appleton, Le Roy H. *American Indian Design and Decoration*. Dover Publications, Inc., 1971.

Caduto, Michael J., and Bruchac, Joseph. *Keepers of the Earth*: *Native American Stories & Environmental Activities for Children*. Fulcrum Inc., 1988.

Finney, Susan, and Kindle, Patricia. *American Indians: Independent Learning Units*. Good Apple Inc., 1985.

Grun, Bernard. *The Timetables of History,* 3rd rev. ed. Simon and Schuster, 1991.

Schuman, Jo Miles. *Art from Many Hands*. Davis Publications, Inc., 1981.

Walters, Anna Lee. *The Spirit of Native America: Beauty and Mysticism in American Indian Art*. Chronicle Books, 1989.

For Students

Baker, Olaf. *Where the Buffaloes Begin.* Frederick Warne, 1981.

Baylor, Byrd. *Hawk, I'm Your Brother.* Aladdin Books, 1976.

———. *When Clay Sings.* Charles Scribner's Sons, 1972.

Cohlene, Terri. *Quillworker: A Cheyene Legend.* Watermill Press, 1990.

Dancing Teepees: Poems of American Indian Youth; selected by Virginia H. Sneve. Holiday House, 1989.

DePaola, Tomie. *The Legend of the Bluebonnet.* G. P. Putnam's Sons, 1983.

DePaola, Tomie. *The Legend of the Indian Paintbrush.* G. P. Putnam's Sons, 1988.

Goble, Paul. *The Girl Who Loved Wild Horses.* Bradbury Press, 1986.

Jassem, Kate. *Chief Joseph: Leader of Destiny.* Troll Associates, 1979.

Jeffers, Susan. *Brother Eagle, Sister Sky: A Message from Chief Seattle.* Dial Books, 1991.

Martin, Bill Jr., and Archambault, John. *Knots on a Counting Rope.* Henry Holt & Co. Inc., 1987.

McLain, Gary. *The Indian Way—Learning to Communicate with Mother Nature.* John Muir Publications, 1990.

Rodanas, Kristina. *Dragonfly's Tale.* Clarion Books, 1991.

The Elements and Principles of Design

Patchwork in Harmony

> "*Their quilts were journals in cloth on which they could focus their remembrances.*"
>
> *Patricia Cooper & Norma Bradley Allen, authors of The Quilters*

Basic Training in Design

Someone once said that if a work of art is like a pie, the ingredients are the elements of design. The directions for putting the ingredients together, then, are the principles of composition. These directions are the foundation for what makes a design work. In this section, traditional colonial patchwork patterns are used to introduce the vocabulary and concepts of design study. They also illustrate the timeless appeal of good design.

A formal study of art will often return to the elements and principles when planning (or viewing) a composition. This doesn't mean there is a formula for great art; it means there are some consistent guidelines to consider. A few people are able to intuitively arrange a brilliant design; they have a rare gift. The majority of us must slowly and thoughtfully learn to control the elements, to have them work to successfully express whatever is intended.

STEP 6.

The paper quilt may be finished with a ruffle by using 3" strips of crepe paper. Just pleat and glue around the outside perimeter.

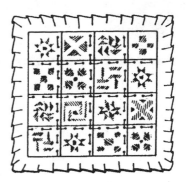

Suggestion: Serve apple cider and gingerbread (being careful of any food sensitivities individuals may have), explaining the concept of a quilting bee and telling students that these were the refreshments often served.

Integrating Ideas

The paper patchwork quilt can be one of many activities incorporated into a colonial unit. For example:

- The class can be divided into groups to research the northern, middle, and southern colonies. Invite students to brainstorm questions they would like to know about colonial life. Also have them think about:

    a. What was the origin of the people who lived in these colonies?

    b. What was the landscape and the architecture like?

    c. How did people make a living?

    d. Who were some of the important leaders?

    e. What were the schools like?

    f. What did adults and children do for fun?

    g. Describe a typical colonial day.

- Students can create murals and dioramas depicting what they've learned.

- Invite groups to give presentations to the class, comparing the varying lifestyles of the colonies. Speculation can be made as to the types of problems, if any, that might occur because of the variations.

- Have a Colonial Celebration as a culminating activity. Groups of students rotate among stations that involve putting together the paper patchwork quilt, dipping candles, making braided rugs, baking bread, using a spinning wheel, playing colonial games, experimenting with natural dyes on handkerchiefs, and so forth. Some of these activities may require close teacher supervision.

- The patchwork quilt design can also be used when studying pioneers or geometry.

Books

For Teachers and Parents

Carratello, John, and Carratello, Patty. *Revolutionary War.* Teacher Created Materials. Huntington Beach, CA, 1991.

Cheatham, Frank; Cheatham Jane; and Haler, Sheryl. *Design Concepts and Applications.* Prentice-Hall, Inc., 1983.

Copeland, Peter F. *Early American Trades Coloring Book.* Dover Publishers Inc., 1980.

Linderman, Marlene. *Art in the Elementary School: Drawing, Painting, and Creating for the Classroom.* rev. ed. Wm. C. Brown Publishers, 1984.

Syme, Lynette Merlin. *Learning Patchwork.* Sterling Publishing, 1987.

For Students

Cohen, Barbar. *Molly's Pilgrim.* A Bantam Skylark Book, 1983.

MacLachlan, Patricia. *Sarah, Plain and Tall.* Harper & Row, Publishers, 1985.

McGovern, Ann. *If You Sailed on the Mayflower.* Four Winds Press, 1985.

Mitsumasa, Anno. *Anno's USA.* Philomel Books, 1983.

Paul, Ann. *Eight Hands Round: A Patchwork Alphabet.* HarperCollins, 1991.

Penner, Lucile Recht. *Eating the Plates.* Macmillan Publishing Co., 1991.

Polacco, Patricia. *The Keeping Quilt.* Simon & Schuster, 1988.

Purdy, Carol. *Iva Dunnit and the Big Wind.* Dial Books, 1985.

Ringgold, Faith. *Tar Beach.* Crown Publishers Inc., 1991.

Shaw, Janet B. *Meet Kirsten: An American Girl.* Scholastic Inc., 1986.

Wilder, Laura Ingalls. *Little House in the Big Woods.* Scholastic Inc., 1960.

The Nature of Color Vision

Early in the 19th century, the painter Eugene Delacroix made some observations about color that he recorded in his diary. He wrote that pure colors are rare in nature, everything appears with varied tone, shading, and reflection. Delacroix's ideas plus research by color scientists led to the interest in color and light experienced during the great decade of Impressionism (1870–1880). Impressionist experiments became a reference for modern color theory. This important movement in the visual arts has influenced the style and use of color for many contemporary painters.

In his study of color, Delacroix noticed that the shadow cast by a colored object will contain a tinge of the opposite color. This idea was a principle element in Impressionist paintings. Purple shadows painted among the green grass or shades of blue brushed on the surface of skin illustrated (and exaggerated) the relative nature of color. Color is not an absolute reality. What the eye perceives is affected by light and color in the environment. The way the eye responds is part of the visual experience. The human eye demands a balance of color sensations. When balance is absent, the eye becomes fatigued and adjusts by creating the vision of the opposite color. This phenomenon is called *simultaneous contrast*.

Experiments in Simultaneous Contrast

Take a sheet of red and a sheet of green construction paper (about 8 1/2" x 11"). Cut out two pieces of gray construction paper, 2" square. Set a gray square in the center of each colored sheet.

Place the red sheet in direct light and gaze at the gray area (without blinking) for a minute or two. When the eye becomes fatigued the gray square will take on a blue-green tinge. The gray square on green will look faintly red-violet.

Next, cut two small pieces of purple construction paper (2" square). Place one in the center of an orange sheet of paper and the other in the center of a green sheet of paper. Place the green and orange sheets next to each other and compare the appearance of the two purple squares. The purple area on the orange sheet will appear more blue, while the purple on green will appear more red.

Color Relationships

> *"All colors are the friends of their neighbors and the lovers of their opposites."*
>
> *Marc Chagall*

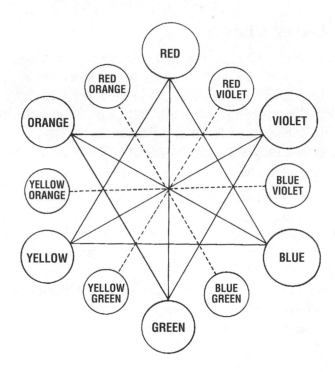

The **hue chart** is used when planning a color composition. It is arranged in a circle to show the relationships between the twelve pure colors in the color spectrum.

Color Qualities

Every color has three qualities: hue, intensity, and value. The infinite range of color that we see can be traced to a variation of these qualities. Color can be altered by combining two adjacent hues; each hue can vary from bright to dull (intensity) and from light to dark (value). A color that is red in hue can be either bright or dull red, and it can also be light or dark red.

HUE

Each distinctively different color on the previous chart is known as a *hue*. There are hundreds of colors but only twelve hues. The colors next to each other are *adjacent* hues; the opposite color is the *complement*. (It is this opposite that the eye sees with simultaneous contrast.)

INTENSITY

Each color can be described as a high, medium, or low intensity hue. *High* intensity hues are the bright, pure colors that appear in the spectrum. *Low* intensity is the dull hue tone just before it becomes neutral. For example, bright orange is a high intensity hue. At low intensity it becomes brown. *Medium* intensity is halfway in-between.

VALUE

A single hue can have several distinct levels of value. To simplify this introduction, these levels will be described as *light, medium,* and *dark* values. The pure colors of the hue chart also have different values. Bright violet is darker than bright red and bright red is darker than bright yellow.

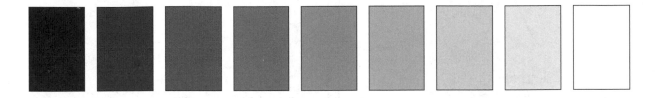

Describing Color

Look around and identify the color qualities of everyday items. For example, the color of pink lemonade can be described as high intensity (bright) red hue with light value. (Since the value is light, red becomes pink.)

THE COLOR OF	HUE	INTENSITY	VALUE
Grape Jam	Violet	High	Dark
Pink Lemonade	Red	High	Light
Chocolate	Orange	Low	Medium or Dark
Peanut Butter	Yellow-Orange	Low	Medium
Margarine	Yellow	Medium	Light
Pickles	Green	Medium	Medium

Color Composition

The rules of composition are universal and unchanging. Throughout history, some of the finest examples of decorative or expressive use of color have had a similar structure. Color structure is based on **order** and **balance**. These concepts organize the element of color to create visual unity.

Look at attractive color arrangements in fabric, interior design, and fine art. Notice that one color group will usually dominate the total area. This **dominant group** establishes order with a single hue or group of related hues within a limited range of intensity and value. The remaining colors oppose (give relief from) the dominant group and create balance. The **color balance** (or *related-variation*) must relate to one or more of the dominant qualities of hue, intensity, or value.

From *Art Connections*, published by GoodYearBooks. Copyright © 1995 Kimberly Boehler Thompson and Diana Standing Loftus.

Observe the *Mona Lisa* by Leonardo da Vinci. This painting is a masterpiece of color composition.

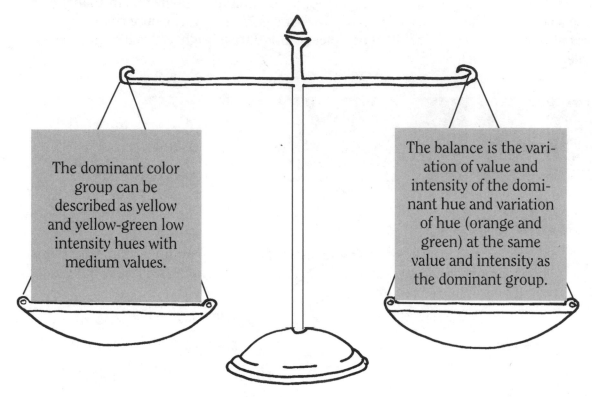

The dominant color group can be described as yellow and yellow-green low intensity hues with medium values.

The balance is the variation of value and intensity of the dominant hue and variation of hue (orange and green) at the same value and intensity as the dominant group.

To illustrate the importance of order and balance in this composition, imagine what would happen if Mona Lisa had bright red lips and fingernails. The eye, instead of moving comfortably throughout the composition, would continually return and stop at the areas of unrelated color.

High intensity hues can be used in low intensity color schemes if they are related in some way. Bright colors, however, have more visual weight than low intensity colors, and should be used in small amounts or the composition will appear out of balance.

The more neutral a color (as it loses intensity), the easier it is to balance in a color scheme. An extreme example is black and white. These two colors are perfectly neutral and can be used in any color arrangement. Gray can be used freely except if the values of the dominant color group are medium. Then the gray values should be medium as well.

With observation and experimentation, the structure of color will become clear.

Project

Composition with Fractions

Materials

- 12" x 18" black or white construction paper
- construction paper in a variety of colors
- pencil
- ruler
- compass
- scissors
- paste or glue

Procedure

STEP 1.

Discuss color theory with the class. Talk about adjacent and complementary colors, color qualities, and the importance of order and balance in composition.

STEP 2.

Help students plan a design using fractions of the spectrum. Using the hue chart and the following examples, select three related colors of construction paper. Two of the colors should be neighbors (*adjacent*) on the chart or fairly close to to each other. The third color should be the opposite (*complement*) of either adjacent color. In this color scheme, one of the adjacent colors will be called the dominant hue. (The color adjacent to the dominant and the complement is the hue balance.)

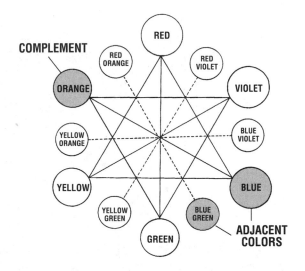

STEP 3.

Using a compass with a 2" radius, have students draw a total of 6 circles (4" in diameter) on the three sheets of construction paper—3 circles in the dominant hue, 2 circles in the adjacent hue, and 1 circle in the complementary hue.

STEP 4.

Demonstrate how to divide the colored circles into fractions using the following method. The compass with the same 2" radius can be used to mark the perimeter of a circle equally at 6 points. This will locate the diameter of all the circles and help divide four of the circles into 2, 3, 6, and 12 sections. The division of the other two circles into 4 and 8 sections can be estimated by sight or the circles can be cut out and the sections divided by folding.

STEP 5.

Cut out all the colored circles. Cut them into the following fractions: dominant hue: divide 1 circle in half, 1 circle in fourths, and 1 circle in eighths; adjacent hue: divide 1 circle into thirds and 1 circle into sixths; complementary hue: divide the 1 circle into twelve equal sections.

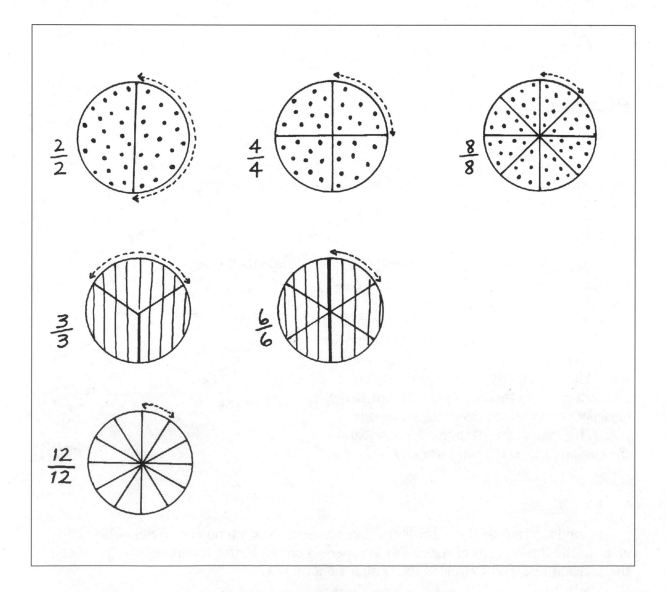

STEP 6.

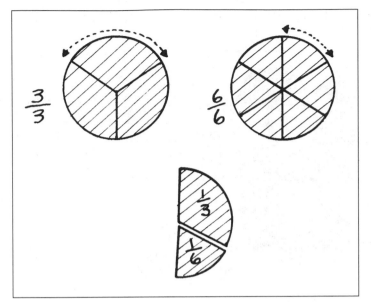

Ask students to discover which combination of fractions in each color are equal to 1/2 circle (such as 3/6 or 1/3 + 1/6). Then have them choose a combination of sections and remove half of the circle from each color. Set these pieces aside. They will be left out of the composition.

STEP 7.

Have students determine the remaining amount of each color to be used in the fraction design. (dominant color–2 1/2 circles, adjacent color–1 1/2 circles, and complementary color–1/2 circle.)

STEP 8.

Give everyone a 12" x 18" sheet of black or white paper and have them arrange the fractions of color until they are happy with a design. Glue the pieces in place.

VARIATION:

Use fractions of different geometric shapes for a similar color composition.

Game

Color Identification

The chart earlier in the lesson illustrates how to describe color. All the colors in the world can be described by their hue, their intensity, and their value. Students can practice defining color with self-made flash cards.

Cut out color examples from magazine pages or fabric scraps. Glue these onto index cards. Display each card. Have students describe the colors, stating hue, intensity, and value. A matching game can also be used with the flash cards. To do this, have color descriptions that match the color card written on separate index cards.

Integrating Ideas

- Have students brainstorm ways to use fractions in everyday life. (For example, measurement, cooking, tools, money, and telling time.)

- Two excellent resources for teaching fractions are listed below under "Books." They are *About Teaching Mathematics: A K–8 Resource* by Marilyn Burns and *Mathematics: A Way of Thinking* by Robert Baratta-Lorton. The creative activities suggested in these books are not only fun and challenging; they also provide students with concrete, hands-on ways of understanding fractions.

Books

For Teachers and Parents

Baratta-Lorton, Robert. *Mathematics: A Way of Thinking.* Addison-Wesley Publishing Company, 1977.

Burns, Marilyn. *About Teaching Mathematics: A K–8 Resource.* Marilyn Burns, Education Associates. Sausalito, California. Distributed by Cuisenaire Co. of America. White Plains, New York, 1992.

Pappas, Theoni. *Mathematics Appreciation.* Wide World Publishing, 1986.

Seymour, Dale, and Britton, Jill. *Introduction to Tessellations.* Dale Seymour Publications, 1989.

For Students

Crews, Donald. *Freight Train.* Morrow, 1985.

Emberley, Ed. *Picture Pie.* Little Brown & Co., 1984.

Jenkins, Jessica. *Thinking About Colors.* Dutton Children's Books, 1992.

Greeley, Valerie. *White Is the Moon.* Macmillan Publishing Co., 1990.

Lionni, Leo. *A Color of His Own.* Pantheon Books, 1975.

McMillan, Bruce. *Eating Fractions.* Scholastic Inc., 1991.

Munsch, Robert, and Desputeaux, Helene. *Purple, Green and Yellow.* Annick Press Ltd., 1992.

O'Neill, Mary. *Hailstones and Halibut Bones: Adventure in Color.* Doubleday & Co. Inc., 1989.

Raboff, Ernest. *Art for Children.* Harper and Row, 1987–1988. (Series includes masters of color such as: Leonardo da Vinci, Rembrandt, Van Gogh, and Henri Matisse.)

Evaluation Is An Inside Job

Art education provides an understanding of art concepts, production, and history. This background helps us to evaluate and make decisions about our own artwork and the things we see in the world around us. The ability to evaluate is valuable to individual creative growth. It is a learning tool and, at best, an inside job.

A critical evaluation is a judgment made about the quality, success, or value of a finished work of art. Even with technical knowledge and historical perspective, these decisions are difficult to make. Standards of excellence in art change constantly and judgments are often subjective. Value is ultimately decided by how an expert feels about the work. In the arts, a critical evaluation is an educated opinion.

Self-evaluation is a process that shapes the creative experience. It can open the door to problem solving by raising questions before, during, and after a project. These questions help students to visualize, organize, and analyze. This will improve the quality of any work, develop self-discipline, and teach flexibility.

To creative thinkers, the questions are more important than the answers. Henry James said ". . . our doubt is our passion and our passion is our task."

There are different questions for each stage of a project. They can be remembered as **prepare** (before), **pause** (during), and **ponder** (after).

Prepare

 he first step is to relax and think.

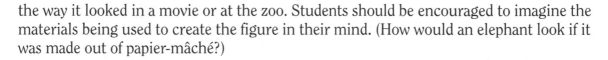

What do I know about this material?

What are the characteristics? This is a reality question. For example, if a student is going to make a papier-mâché elephant, it is helpful for him or her to know what papier-mâché looks like before forming expectations about his or her own work. This may seem elementary, but the goal of a student without experience is often to re-create a figure the way it looked in a movie or at the zoo. Students should be encouraged to imagine the materials being used to create the figure in their mind. (How would an elephant look if it was made out of papier-mâché?)

What kinds of problems might there be?

Problems are just unexpected questions. If a person has experienced problems in the past, that person has valuable experience. Foreseeing a problem prepares us to solve it. Then it is either prevented or becomes just another question.

How do I want my work to look?

Students will be more satisfied with the results of their work if they are taught to visualize before they start. They can't reach a goal if they don't know what that goal is; they can't draw a beautiful flower if they don't have their own concept of beautiful. Help them begin the picture in their mind by studying examples of their subject. What is the most beautiful flower that I can imagine? Where is it? What is the time of day? What are the colors? How do different artists draw flowers? These questions can be adapted and generalized to any object. What is my favorite animal? Why do I find elephants interesting? If I could, how would I make an elephant more interesting?

Pause

reating and evaluating do not take place at the same time. Take a break and take a look (review).

Does the work look the way I imagined it?

Visualization in the preparation stage helps to make decisions about subject, design, color, and technique. It is used to start the creative process rather than determine what the end results will be. Work that is creative, more often than not, is the result of an idea that has been allowed to develop. If the work doesn't look "quite right" it may be that the student is trying too hard to make the image exactly the way it looked in his or her mind.

What do I like about the work?

Evaluate a work in progress frequently. Try to see it from a different point of view. Hold the piece in front of a mirror, upside-down, dim the lights, or wait an hour and look at it again. What areas are the most interesting? Why? Are there unexpected things happening that I like? These are clues that help decide how to continue. Build with the elements that are working.

What can I improve?

The *Serenity Prayer* by Reinhold Niebuhr puts into words the best evaluation state of mind. "Grant me the Serenity to accept the things I cannot change; Courage to change the things I can; and Wisdom to know the difference."

Every work has its problems and any area that is not successful is a question. Does the shape need adjustment? Is the color too dull? Sometimes it's enough to recognize the problem, leave it, and move ahead. At other times, the student may decide to make a change. Changes should be made in the same relaxed way that work begins, with questions about the materials, challenges, and possibilities.

I've made a mistake. What can I do?

An insightful art teacher once told his students that to be artists they must first make 100 mistakes. Keep in mind the quote by Edward Phelps: "The person who makes no mistakes does not usually make anything." A flaw can become an asset. A hole in a painting can be a window and paint splatters can be fireworks. If the painting is ruined, it can still be an important lesson.

Marcel Duchamp, one of the original Dada artists, made a wire and plate glass construction in 1915 and left it unfinished. In 1926 it was accidentally broken. When Duchamp repaired "The Large Glass," he left the cracks in so the piece would be considered finished by chance. Today this is considered his major work. (The Dada art movement sprang from critical attitudes toward our society after World War I. The artists responded with works that were both playful and absurd.)

Is the work finished?

Paul Gardner, an American contemporary artist, once said "A painting is never finished, it simply stops in interesting places." Part of the skill in any art form is knowing when to stop. Enthusiastic students often overwork an idea because they fall in love with the process. (This is only a problem if the student is then disappointed with his composition.) Time should be scheduled at the end of an art experience to relax and look for signs of resolution in the work.

Ponder

A successful experience includes a few minutes to respond and reflect.

- ◉ How did I feel while I was working?
- ◉ Am I satisfied?
- ◉ What do I want to remember for the next time?
- ◉ What would I do differently?

Every activity that involves production is an opportunity to introduce students to the evaluation process. We must not mislead them into thinking they are merely looking for answers when they are, in reality, looking for more important questions. In this way, art mirrors life.

From *Art Connections*, published by GoodYearBooks. Copyright © 1995 Kimberly Boehler Thompson and Diana Standing Loftus.

Collage

Social Images

Collage as a Medium of Self-Expression

This is an excellent lesson to begin the year because it fosters a climate of self-awareness and acceptance. By creating a collage of themselves, students focus on who they are, their dreams, and their interests. If possible, make one of yourself ahead of time. Not only will it provide a good model, but students will have a chance to learn more about you.

Collage is an exercise in composition. Through their creation, students experience the role of color, shape, positive and negative space, and texture. The lessons on Color Theory and Design will be a helpful reference.

A Little History

Collage is a French word meaning pasting paper. The first known use of this technique was by Japanese calligraphers in the twelfth century. They copied poems onto sheets covered with pasted pieces of softly tinted paper. The elegant compositions were then sprinkled with tiny shapes cut from gold and silver paper. A similar tradition of combining text and collage has lived on in Japan, where holiday greetings are often still written on pasted paper.

Cutting and pasting was used artistically by western Europeans in the seventeenth century to assemble and illustrate beautiful family albums. By the middle of the eighteenth century, English speaking countries applied the technique to valentines. So, it can be said that love pushed the limits of collage even further. Leaves, flowers, locks of hair, gold filigree, tiny dolls, and a variety of objects were often attached to the cards to express affection.

In the fine arts, collage first appeared in Cubist paintings. *Cubism* was an early twentieth-century artistic style based on the experiments of Pablo Picasso and Georges Braque. Forms were reduced to abstract, geometric shapes, often depicting several views of the same subject. Occasionally, these shapes were cut and pasted next to painted forms. Printed papers and other actual objects were sometimes added to the paintings.

Pablo Picasso. *Guitar*. Céret (after March, 1913). Pasted paper, charcoal, ink and chalk on blue paper mounted on ragboard, 26 1/8 x 19 1/2". The Museum of Modern Art, New York. Nelson A. Rockefeller Bequest.

Project

Self-Portrait Collage

Students should be encouraged to use materials that reflect their ideas and interests. They may enjoy choosing photos, magazine pictures, and other favorite items. The challenge is to create a composition with visual unity out of a collection of treasures.

Materials

- a backing sheet of posterboard, tagboard or other sturdy surface to support the composition
- interesting collage items such as feathers, photos, ribbons, buttons, leaves, and so on
- construction paper
- gift wrap or wallpaper
- magazines
- fabric
- scissors
- glue or paste

Preparation

Prepare students for the collage experience by showing them related compositions. Many well-known artists have made art with nonart materials. Some of these artists use collage which, by definition, means that the materials are fastened with paste or glue. Pictures may be found in most books on art of the twentieth century or modern art. Look for examples of work by Kurt Schwitters, Romare Bearden, Arthur Dove, Jean Dubuffet, and Louise Nevelson.

Interesting ideas for collage composition may also be sparked by artwork that is not collage. Topics to consider are: Pop Art, Dada, or Surrealism; paintings by Picasso, Piet Mondrian, or Stuart Davis; and the paper cutouts of Henri Matisse.

Procedure

Understanding composition comes from studying fine artwork carefully and often. If possible, students should be given visual tours through books, art galleries, or museums. While looking at examples, discuss the collage elements of color, texture, shape, and positive and negative space. This can be an introduction (or review) to design elements.

(See Design pp. 26–33 and Color pp. 34–43) Get philosophical; talk order, balance, rhythm, and the principles of composition. Be brave; if it was easy to translate the visual language into words, many artists would write instead of draw, paint, or sculpt.

Selecting the Design Elements

STEP 1. COLOR

Have students look at their collected objects to see if there is a dominant color among them (other than black and white). If there is a lot of variety, instruct them to decide on a color group to emphasize. (A color group is a range of related colors–different shades and tones of red, blue, or yellow, and so on.) Then invite them to choose colored papers or fabrics that will help develop their color scheme.

Next, have students lay all of their collage objects and materials out on different colored sheets of tagboard or posterboard. This is the surface of the collage. Rather than choosing a favorite color, tell students to select a background that will enhance the composition.

STEP 2. TEXTURE

Texture is an element, like color, that can add interest to a design. Pinecones, feathers, and fabric give the collage texture. Printed paper such as gift wrap and wallpaper can also be used for "visual" texture.

Have students look at the kinds of texture–coarse, irregular, even, or smooth–that can be found in their collage collection. Then ask them to choose related textures or patterns that will compliment the items. Tell students to let their eyes decide what looks good together. Invite them to add these to their supply of materials.

STEP 3. SHAPE

Using their original collection of objects, instruct students to determine the most common shape. Are the items mainly geometric (squares, circles, and so on) or organic (shapes from nature)?

Reminding students to keep the principles of repetition and variation in mind, invite them to begin cutting into the selection of papers and fabrics. Have them pull the arrangement together with different sizes of related shapes. Suggest altering some of the shapes for variation. The background shape can be made more interesting by cutting into a few areas or by extending elements beyond the collage border.

STEP 4. LINE

Line often exists as a result of other elements. It can organize the composition, create rhythm, and express feeling. To add more line to the composition, invite students to experiment with varieties of yarn, wire, string, or even dried pasta.

Have students lay the linear materials out with the other objects. Suggest they try different line arrangements (and directions) such as repeated, alternating, radiating, and random. Invite them to experiment with the expressive qualities of smooth, straight, thin, jagged, and bold.

STEP 5. POSITIVE AND NEGATIVE SPACE

There are two kinds of space in the composition: **positive space** (the dominant shapes), and **negative space** (the surrounding area). As the arrangement of the positive elements begins to develop, tell students to pay attention to the color, texture, and shape of the negative space. This area is also an important part of the composition. It can either reflect the main elements or make them prominent by contrast.

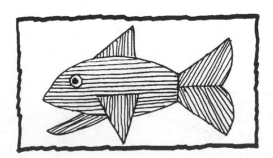

Planning the Composition

<u>STEP 6.</u>

When planning the collage, remind students that repeated colors, textures, and shapes will organize the composition and tie it together visually. Variation of these elements makes them stand out. Both of these principles are valuable to a balanced arrangement. Too much variety and our eyes become confused; too much order and the viewer becomes bored.

Have students examine their different collage elements and begin their arrangement. While deciding on the placement of colors, textures, and shapes, invite them to look for rhythm in the design. Rhythm brings the eye into the composition and lets it move comfortably throughout to see the different, but related objects. When they are satisfied with what they see, have students fasten the materials in place.

> *" . . . not chaos-like together crushed and bruised, But, as the world, harmoniously confused: Where order in variety we see, And where, though all things differ, all agree."*
>
> *Alexander Pope, (Windsor Forest)*

Integrating Ideas

- ☻ Ask students to consider the following questions: "What is it about my life that makes me a unique, special individual?" "What do I like most about my life and think about most often?"
- ☻ Display the finished collages on a bulletin board.
- ☻ Each week, choose a different student to be the class V.I.P. Set aside time during the week to spend with that student. Arrange a time during the week for the V.I.P. to share his or her collage and anything else brought from home. Have each student write a positive note to the V.I.P. Collect the notes, put them together into a booklet, and give them to the V.I.P. This activity can help students better know and understand themselves and each other and appreciate each other's differences and feelings.
- ☻ Collage can also be used as a creative way to show information learned from current events, research, or a favorite book.

Books

For Teachers and Parents

Fletcher, Ruth. *Teaching Peace. Skills for Living in a Global Society.* Harper and Row, 1986.

Kostic, Diane. *The Biography of Me: A Journey of Self-Discovery.* Good Apple, 1992.

Lipson, Greta Barclay, and Romatowski, Jane A. *Ethnic Pride.* Good Apple Inc., 1983.

Roukes, Nicholas. *Art Synectics.* Davis Publications, 1982.

For Students

Baylor, Byrd. *I'm in Charge of Celebrations.* Charles Scribner's Sons, 1986.

Blume, Judy. *Freckle Juice.* A Yearling Book, 1971.

If I Were in Charge of the World; poems by Judith Viorst. Aladdin Books, 1981.

Raboff, Ernest. *Henri Matisse.* Harper and Row, 1988.

———. *Pablo Picasso.* Harper and Row, 1987.

Rylant, Cynthia. *When I Was Young in the Mountains.* E. P. Dutton, 1982.

Spier, Peter. *People.* Doubleday, 1980.

Drawing Techniques

Visualizing Animal Characteristics

> *"I had to create an equivalent for what I felt about what I was looking at— not copy it."*
>
> *Georgia O'Keeffe, American artist, 1887-1986*

Using Drawing as a Means of Taking a Closer Look at Animals

The drawing techniques taught in this lesson include warm-up exercises and different ways of seeing art. Using these methods, students analyze and compare animal characteristics.

A Little History

Drawing is both unique and fundamental to human communication. The walls of ancient caves have preserved evidence of early man's ability to represent the world with lines, marks, and shapes. These artists frequently drew with chunks of red and yellow ocher. Their subjects were often animals. The animals are shown in natural poses and are often surrounded by hunting symbols. Because some of the rock surfaces have been chipped, it is theorized that ancient people may have thrown their spears at the drawings. In 1942, one of the most fantastic discoveries of prehistoric art occurred. The discovery happened by accident. In the Dordogne region of France at Lascaux, two young boys and their dog were playing. The boys followed their dog into a hole. The hole led them into caves that had been sealed for thousands of years. Once inside, the boys lit a match. Wonderful drawings of animals were illuminated on the walls. The drawings the boys found were over 10,000 years old. We can only speculate on the purpose and meaning of this ancient art but through it, amateurs and professionals all over the world continue to uncover clues from the past.

Projects

Approaches to Drawing

Materials

- pencil
- colored pencil
- felt-tipped pens (water-base ink)
- chalk
- pastels
- charcoal
- white drawing paper

Preparation

Setting Up the Classroom Environment for Drawing

Drawing is language, a means of gathering and communicating information. Each of us has a unique "voice" that we must learn to control and project. Drawing ability can be built on a foundation of these four basic needs:

- Students need to be influenced, to study and copy great works of art. They should see drawings by Leonardo da Vinci, Toulouse-Lautrec, Paul Klee, Kathe Kollwitz, and Ben Shahn.
- They need to be introduced to techniques, tools, and quality materials, and shown how to apply them.
- They need to learn how to "see" with lessons that show them the structure of things.
- They need to feel safe in a nonjudgmental environment that encourages exploration.

Warm-Up Exercises

Before beginning to draw, the artist should get comfortable. Invite students to sit at a table or desk and relax their arms, neck, legs, and feet. Suggest they find their most relaxed upright posture. (Any time they start to feel tense while drawing, tell them to return to this position.) Now begin warm-up exercises to loosen up the hand. This is a time to introduce students to different drawing techniques. It is also an opportunity for students to think about an image they would like to draw and plan how to develop it.

STEP 1

Allow students to choose a drawing medium and experiment with different lines, shapes, and techniques for texture or shading. Invite them to change the pressure of the drawing tool and try holding it at various angles. Suggest they place the drawing tool on its side and drag or twist it to draw. Students can explore smearing and softening techniques by rubbing pencil or chalk lines with cotton swabs or cotton balls. Tell them to let their hand and mind wander. They should scribble or doodle freely and not erase.

Lines—straight, curved, jagged, wavy, bold, thin

Shapes—circle, oval, square, triangle, organic, figurative

Textures or Shading Techniques—dots (stippling), dashes (hatching, crosshatching)

STEP 2

At first, drawings should be loose and random. Gradually instruct students to use more hand control to make lines that are even and flowing. Have them develop the shapes into shaded forms. Tell them to imagine a light source coming from one direction in their drawing and use different techniques to darken the shadow side.

Upside-Down Drawing

An exercise to develop perception was introduced by Betty Edwards in *Drawing on the Right Side of the Brain*. Her insight has turned the art of drawing upside-down. Students are given an inverted picture. They are to copy it exactly as it is, inverted. In this position, the image is difficult to recognize and actual seeing is enhanced.

STEP 1.

Have students select a line drawing that is interesting and not too complicated from a book or magazine.

STEP 2.

Invite them to turn it upside-down, concentrate, and draw what they see, beginning at the top of the paper. Tell them to try not to peek at the image right-side-up.

Putting the Pieces Together

Hang a large photograph of an animal where everyone can see it. Have students identify different shapes that make up the figure. Encourage them to describe the space surrounding the animal (the negative space). Help them see different relationships.

Example: Notice that the head of the tiger looks like a triangle attached to the front of a rectangular-shaped body. The negative space beneath the tiger's stomach resembles a crescent moon.

M. Austerman/Animals Animals

STEP 1.

Have the class try to paint the entire picture with shapes, emphasizing any unique or unusual features. Ask them to describe lines and textures and the techniques that can be used to draw details.

STEP 2.

Next, with students sitting comfortably at their desks, and you standing (not so comfortably) at the board, make a quick, light sketch (students using pencil, you using chalk) to plan the size and position of the figure. Instruct students to fill an 8 1/2" x 11" sheet of paper with the drawing or, for smaller drawings, fold the paper in half.

STEP 3.

Everyone should now proceed to draw the animal the way it was described.

If drawing in front of the class makes you feel unsure about your own ability, be honest with the students and willing to learn with them. They will understand and even secretly appreciate the feeling of equality.

At the end of any drawing experience, respond to each student's work individually. Make observations, be positive and encouraging. Avoid comparison; there is no wrong or right way to draw, no better or worse, only different.

Integrating Ideas

To visually connect with animals, make a vertebrate chart using the following method:

a) Each student divides a piece of white drawing paper into 5 sections. Have them write *Vertebrates* across the top. Next, have students add the following headings, one for each box: *Mammals, Amphibians, Reptiles, Fish,* and *Birds.*

b) Have magazines, study prints, filmstrips, library books, and so forth, available for students to gather information about each classification.

c) Have students write several characteristics the animals in each group have in common. Draw examples for each classification.

Books

For Teachers and Parents

Brookes, Mona. *Drawing with Children: A Creative Teaching & Learning Method That Works for Adults, Too.* Jeremy P. Tarcher, Inc., 1986.

Dodson, Bert. *Keys to Drawing.* North Light Books, 1990.

Edwards, Betty. *Drawing on the Right Side of the Brain,* rev. ed., Jeremy P. Tarcher, Inc., 1989.

———. *Drawing on the Artist Within: An Inspirational & Practical Guide to Increasing Your Creative Powers.* Simon and Schuster, Inc., 1987.

Field, Nancy, and Karasov, Corliss. *Discovering Wolves.* Dog Eared Publications, 1991.

Ranger Rick's Naturescope: Amazing Mammals. National Wildlife Federation. Washington, D.C., 1988.

Ranger Rick's Naturescope: Let's Hear It for Herps. National Wildlife Federation. Washington, D.C., 1987.

For Students

Heller, Ruth. *Animals Born Alive and Well.* Scholastic Inc., 1982.

———. *Chickens Aren't the Only Ones.* Scholastic Inc., 1981.

Lionni, Leo. *Fish Is Fish.* Pantheon, 1974.

Raboff, Ernest. *Henri de Toulouse-Lautrec.* Harper and Row, 1988.

———. *Leonardo da Vinci.* Harper and Row, 1987.

———. *Paul Klee.* Harper and Row, 1988.

Richardson, Wendy, and Richardson, Jack. *The Natural World: Through the Eyes of Artists.* Childrens Press, 1991.

Grid Drawing

Scaling a Dinosaur

> "*Every animal leaves traces of what he was; man leaves traces of what he has created.*"
>
> *Jacob Bronowski, author of Ascent of Man*

Using the Grid as a Drawing Tool

This lesson introduces the concepts of scale and proportion. The project is a group activity that combines the study of dinosaurs with an exercise for developing observation and drawing skills.

A Little History

Albrecht Dürer was a great German artist known as the Leonardo da Vinci of the North. In the early 1500s, he envisioned a wire grid device that artists could use to study the proportion and perspective of a figure. The device was placed upright on a drawing table so the model could be seen through it. Drawing paper the same size as the wire grid was marked off with the identical grid pattern. The angles and curves that appeared in each section were copied onto the matching section of the paper. Drawing with this device was difficult because the artist

From *Art Connections*, published by GoodYearBooks. Copyright © 1995 Kimberly Boehler Thompson and Diana Standing Loftus.

had to keep his or her head in exactly the same position or his or her view of the subject would change.

Dürer's grid device illustrated how to re-create the three-dimensional world on a two-dimensional surface. Today the grid is used as a guide for drawing accurate reproductions or enlargements. It is a mechanical technique that provides training in perception. This training prepares students to draw from sight.

Project

Group Grid Drawing

The grid is a visual tool. In this lesson, a grid pattern is drawn onto a picture to focus attention on the lines, curves, and angles of the image. The results of grid drawings are often surprising. This exercise shows that drawing ability is in the eye, not the hand.

Materials

- reproducible dinosaur grid from this lesson
- 88 square pieces of newsprint

or

- a postcard or picture
- ruler
- pencil
- square newsprint or drawing paper for each grid square
- scissors
- tape

Preparation

STEP 1.

Choose a postcard, magazine picture, or photocopy with simple shapes and lines. Use a pencil and ruler to draw an even grid pattern on the picture. Plan the number of squares in the grid so there are one or two for each student to copy. Number each square, then cut the picture into segments following the grid lines.

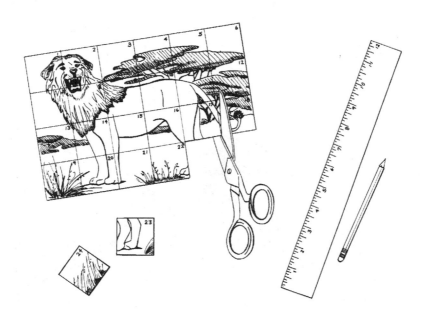

STEP 2.

Cut the drawing paper into square sheets. One sheet is needed for each grid segment of the picture. The size of the drawing paper determines the size of the enlargement. For example, a picture that is 4" x 6" can be divided into 24 sections that are 1" square. If each 1" section is enlarged onto paper that is 12" square, the enlarged pieces will form a 4' x 6' reproduction of the picture.

Procedure

STEP 1.

Give students one or two sections of the picture and a corresponding number of sheets of drawing paper. The grid number should be written on the drawing paper immediately. This will help arrange the picture after the pieces have been enlarged. If a numbered segment of the grid has no portion of the image to copy, a sheet of drawing paper should be given the corresponding number and left blank.

Sighting

STEP 2.

The method used for drawing the copy is called *sighting*. Look at the original picture segment and notice where a line begins, where it ends, and its shape. Mark the relative positions on the large square. Reproduce all lines and shapes as accurately as possible. After the lines have been copied in pencil, color may be added to darken the lines or fill in the shapes.

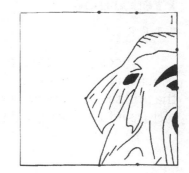

STEP 3.

Assemble the enlargement pieces on a wall. Ask students for their numbered sections in sequence. Position the pieces, tape them in place, and watch the picture unfold.

Visual awareness becomes a special event with this drawing experience. Maps or pictures of other subjects can also be enlarged using these instructions. Try keeping the subject a secret and have students create a mystery enlargement.

Integrating Ideas

◉ Incorporate grid drawing into a unit on dinosaurs. Ask students to guess how long and tall Tyrannosaurus rex was. Use the grid-drawing activity to bring the dinosaur size to life.

◉ Ask students if they can define the word *detective*. Think of examples of detectives from books, television, and movies. Now ask them if they know what a paleontologist is. Discuss the definition. How are the two alike? different?

◉ Have students pretend they are paleontologists. Divide the class into groups. Each group chooses a different dinosaur to research.

◉ Have students write questions they want to know about dinosaurs. Some examples might be: Why are dinosaurs extinct? Which ones were the biggest and smallest? What did they look like? What did they eat? When did they live? What did the landscape look like? How did they care for their young? How did dinosaurs get their names?

- Brainstorm various ways to find out about dinosaurs. Include books, magazines, museums, newspapers, interviews with college professors, filmstrips, and so forth.

- Present dinosaur facts students have learned by using plays, debates, dioramas, murals, writing fiction and nonfiction stories, poems, games, newspaper stories, puppet shows, charts, comic strips, graphs, interviews, maps, etc.

- To challenge thinking further, consider the following questions: 1. How would life be different if dinosaurs were alive today? 2. How would life today be different if dinosaurs had never lived?

- Relate the concept of grid drawing to the idea of everyone doing their part in the grid (or in life) for the picture to become clear. Everyone must work together for the benefit of the whole.

- Grid-drawing techniques could also be used for re-creating the *Mayflower,* maps, self-portraits, or famous paintings.

Books

For Teachers and Parents

Raboff, Ernest. *Art for Children Series.* Harper and Row, 1988.

Ranger Rick's Naturescope: Digging into Dinosaurs. National Wildlife Federation. Washington D.C., 1988.

For Students

Carrick, Carol. *Patrick's Dinosaurs.* Clarion Books/ Ticknor & Fields, 1983.

DePaola, Tomie. *Little Grunt and the Big Egg: A Prehistoric Fairy Tale.* Holiday House, 1990.

Dixon, Dougal. *Hunting the Dinosaurs.* Gareth Stevens, 1987.

Niles, Gregory, and Eldredge, Douglas. *The Fossil Factory: A Kid's Guide to Digging up Dinosaurs, Exploring Evolution, and Finding Fossils.* Addison-Wesley, 1989.

Schlein, Miriam. *Discovering Dinosaur Babies.* Four Winds Press, 1991.

Simon, Seymour. *New Questions and Answers About Dinosaurs.* Morrow Junior Books, 1990.

Yolen, Jane. *Dinosaur Dances.* G. P. Putnam's Sons, 1990.

Yorinks, Arthur. *UGH.* Farrar, Strauss and Giroux, 1990.

Tyrannosaurus rex

se this grid pattern to create an 18' x 22' drawing of a dinosaur.

STEP 1.

Make 2 photocopies of page 67.

STEP 2.

Cut one copy into grid segments. Save only the numbered pieces.

STEP 3.

Cut 88 sheets of newsprint into 18" square pieces.

STEP 4.

Follow project instructions.

STEP 5.

Use the extra photocopy as a guide to reassemble the picture.

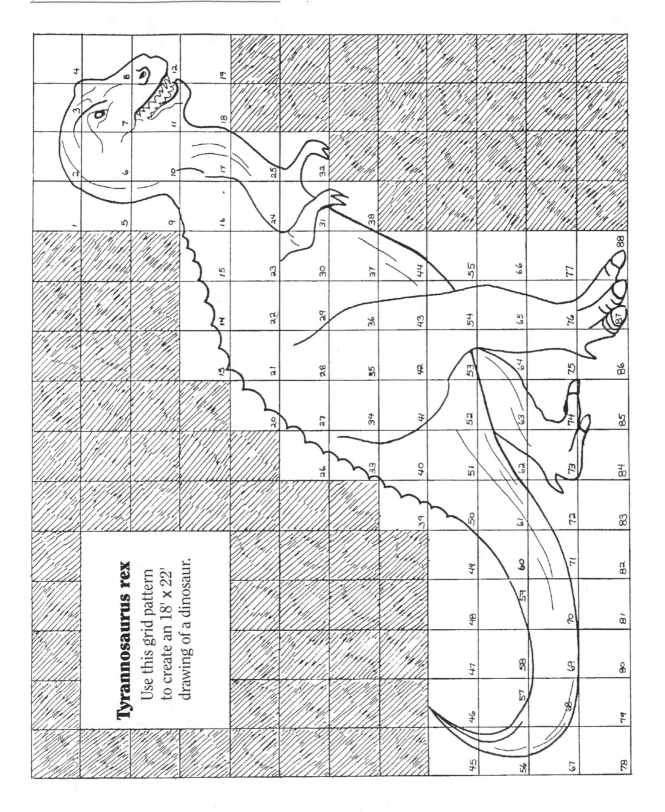

Tyrannosaurus rex

Use this grid pattern to create an 18' x 22' drawing of a dinosaur.

Cartoon Drawing

The Life Cycle in Perspective

> *"I have learned that what I have not drawn, I have never really seen, and that when I start drawing an ordinary thing I realize how extraordinary it is, sheer miracle. . ."*
>
> *Frederick Franck, author of The Zen of Seeing*

Using Cartooning to Get Other Perspectives

Cartoon drawing can be used to develop a more detailed picture of any subject. The project in this lesson introduces basic drawing concepts and ways of bringing cartoon setting and characters to life. Integrating Ideas at the end of the lesson encourages students to imagine and draw the life cycle of a butterfly.

A Little History

Since people first began to communicate, they have expressed their ideas and stories with simple line drawings. The humorous drawings of modern cartoons, however, probably developed as a result of social and technological factors of late 18th century Europe. The social and political climate which invited criticism and satire was often expressed through the arts. Also, advancements in the graphic arts influenced the way the work would look and made it possible to circulate these materials to the public.

Francisco Goya (1746–1828) was a Spanish painter and graphic artist well known for his bitter portrayal of the cruel side of life. His powerful style was to reduce subjects to the essential elements. As a result, he produced caricatures to express his honest vision of man's inhumanity to man. Another popular artist, Honoré Daumier (1808–1879), was known for his dramatic style and social concern. Daumier used light and shadow to transform figures into expressive victims. Motivated by his insight and sympathy for human beings, he created approximately 4,000 drawings that he contributed to various journals for publication.

Project

Creating Your Own Cartoon

Glance at the variety of cartoon styles in any newspaper. Look at the methods that the artists use to illustrate the setting, portray the characters, and express feeling or movement. The message can be presented using exaggeration or suggestion (giving us just a hint).

Materials

- pencil
- colored pencils
- fine point felt-tipped pens
- white drawing paper
- ruler

Procedure

STEP 1.

Tell students that the way to begin a cartoon is by imagining the story they wish to tell.

STEP 2.

Have them choose characters and a setting that will project the mood being created. Any qualities that are important to the story are focused upon. The rest are left out.

From *Art Connections*, published by GoodYearBooks. Copyright © 1995 Kimberly Boehler Thompson and Diana Standing Loftus.

STEP 3.

Invite them to draw their own cartoon, keeping in mind the following information about setting, perspective, and characters.

Drawing the Setting

ome examples of different ways to use location and condition of the setting to enhance the cartoon are:

◎ When the story's location stays the same, the scene can be drawn from different points of view. This makes the sequence interesting.

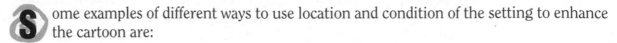

◎ Indicate passing of time by repeating the location and changing the conditions (light to dark, summer to winter).

◎ This technique leaves the details to our imagination. We are shown only the condition of the location (the darkness, the rain, the explosion).

◎ Sequential movement can be illustrated by keeping the location the same and moving the subject, or by changing the location while keeping the subject in position.

The Setting in Perspective

Simple Perspective

To create the illusion of depth in a cartoon setting, consider the following rules of perspective:

◎ Overlapping can be used to show depth.

◎ As things get farther away, they appear smaller.

◎ Objects that are evenly spaced (like fence posts or railroad tracks) appear closer together as they get farther away.

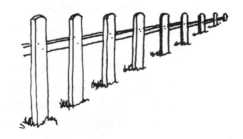

In landscapes, things in the distance appear lighter and less solid.

The Characters

A study of character drawing consists of recognizing the similarities and differences in the way characters look and how they move. With this understanding, students learn to create their own original characters.

Understanding Similarities

Here is a guide for drawing common characteristics. Discuss these and try to think of others.

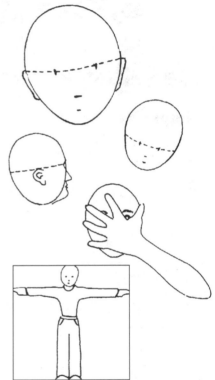

- Heads are often egg-shaped.
- Eyes are about halfway between the top of the head and the chin. A child's eye line is lower than an adults (the younger the child, the lower the eye line) but the nose and mouth are the same.
- The bottom of the nose is about halfway between the eye line and the bottom of the chin.
- The mouth is about halfway between the nose and the chin.
- Looking at the head in profile, the ear is in the center. The top is even with the eye line, the bottom lines up with the tip of the nose.
- The hand of an adult is nearly the same size as the face.
- With arms extended to the side, the distance from fingertip to fingertip is about the same measurement as the person's height.

Compare different types of animals with this guide. Are some of their features similar to ours? Study the characteristics of various characters and describe how to draw them.

Recognizing Differences

A drawing that simplifies the character and exaggerates individual differences is often called a caricature. This style of drawing focuses on the unique qualities that every person, object, or animal has. It may be speckled, fuzzy, wiggly, large, old, or silly. Draw an adult you know, a stuffed animal, or a pet. Notice the distinctive details and try to capture the spirit.

Inventing Characters

The more you know about characters—how they look and how they move—the easier it is to invent new ones. Sometimes, though, it is difficult to begin. Here is a loosening-up exercise to help the cartoonist get started.

Drawing with MMMs.

Draw a light, curved line. Scribble MMMs down the side of it, with the tip of each M touching the line. Erase the curve and let your imagination finish the picture.

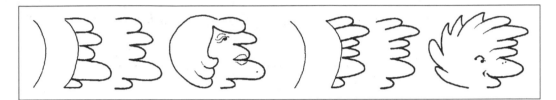

The Character in Motion

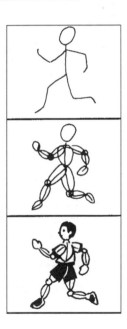

The movement of a cartoon character shows what is happening in the story. It can also show the mood. Cartoonists often exaggerate the activity to make the scene funny or exciting. Look at comic strips to find examples of action illustration.

Learn how to indicate movement by looking at pictures of people and animals in motion. Select one to draw. Begin with lightly sketched lines that represent only the *action* of the figure. These are imaginary action lines. Use them as a guide to draw the figure in the desired position. Develop the main shape using ovals to represent body parts. Add the outline and details.

First practice drawing from pictures. Then attempt live, moving models. Observe the way they bend, sit, turn, and walk. Always try to imagine the action lines.

Integrating Ideas

Cartoon drawing can be used to express the developmental stages of a butterfly.

a) Have students imagine they are a caterpillar egg that is slowly growing and changing into a moving, crawling caterpillar. Ask them to think about what they'll eat and what enemies they'll hide from. Have them recall the day they climbed the milkweed plant and began to spin a cocoon. How did it feel inside the cocoon? What was it like when they became a butterfly and moved their wet wings for the first time? What were they thinking as the sunlight hit their pleated wings and they fluttered about in the air?

From *Art Connections*, published by GoodYearBooks. Copyright © 1995 Kimberly Boehler Thompson and Diana Standing Loftus.

b) After giving them a chance to visualize, take time to discuss the idea of putting part or all of the life cycle into cartoon format.

◉ Depicting major events, retelling a story, illustrating cause and effect, and showing other life cycles are examples of different ways to use cartooning.

> *"What the caterpillar calls the end of the world, the master calls the butterfly."*
>
> *Richard Bach, Illusions: The Adventures of a Reluctant Messiah*

Books

For Teachers and Parents

Jaffe, Roberta, and Appel, Gary. *The Growing Classroom: Garden Based Science.* Addison-Wesley Publishers, 1990.

Meglin, Nick. *The Art of Humorous Illustration.* Watson-Guptill Publications, 1981.

Ranger Rick's Naturescope. Incredible Insects. Discovery Pac. National Wildlife Federation. Washington D.C., 1988.

Roukes, Nicholas. *Design Synectics.* Davis Publications, 1988.

Tolman, Marvin N., and Morton, James O. *Life Science Activities for Grades 2–8.* Parker Publishing Co. Inc., 1986.

For Students

Brinckloe, Julie. *Fireflies!* Aladdin Books, 1985.

Carle, Eric. *The Very Hungry Caterpillar.* Philomel Books, 1987.

Cox, Rosamund Kidman, and Cork, Barbara Usborne. *Butterflies and Moths.* First Nature Books, 1990.

Fleischman, Paul. *Joyful Noise.* Harper & Row, 1988.

Heller, Ruth. *How to Hide a Butterfly and Other Insects.* Platt and Munk All Aboard Books, 1992.

Howe, James. *I Wish I Were a Butterfly.* Harcourt Brace Jovanovich, 1987.

Mellonie, Bryan, and Ingpen, Robert. *Lifetimes.* Bantam, 1983.

O'Neill, Dan; O'Neill, Marian; and O'Neill, Hugh D., Jr. *The Big Yellow Drawing Book.* Hugh O'Neill and Associates, 1988.

Schulz, Charles M. *Charlie Brown, Snoopy and Me.* Doubleday & Co. Inc., 1980.

Silverstein, Shel. *Lafcadio, the Lion Who Shot Back.* Harper and Row, 1963.

Paper Making

Recycling is Our Future

> *"Civilization no longer needs to open up wilderness; it needs to help open up the still largely unexplored mind."*
>
> *David Rains Wallace, American writer, born 1945*

Using Paper Making to Illustrate Recycling

In this lesson, students are given the opportunity to experience the transformation of pulp into hand-made paper. Not only do they explore the significance of preserving trees, they will gain insight into the recycling process. Instructions for reusable paper-making sets are included in the lesson.

Paper can be made from many different plant fibers. Wood is the most common source of fiber but cotton or linen rags are often used to create paper of the finest quality.

Paper exists in many forms, from the cereal box on the breakfast table to the book we read at night. Most of what we use has been made by machine. It can be ordinary or luxurious, with a variety of characteristics—silky, rough, light, stiff, or airy.

Artists must consider how the different qualities of paper can affect the appearance and permanence of their

From *Art Connections*, published by GoodYearBooks. Copyright © 1995 Kimberly Boehler Thompson and Diana Standing Loftus.

work. Many still insist on using only handmade paper, which they purchase or make themselves. There are few materials as beautiful as a well-crafted sheet of paper. When touched by sensitive hands, the paper itself becomes a work of art.

A Little History

By the time man discovered the process, paper had already existed in the insect world for several million years. The original paper makers were probably wasps. Wasps use a paper-making process to build their nests. They chew wood and plant fibers and mix this material with saliva. Then they shape the pulp and let it dry. When the nest is finished, it is actually a paper product.

The history of man-made paper began over 2000 years ago. Some experts believe the process was invented in China about A.D.105 by a man named Ts'ai Lun. Others believe that Ts'ai Lun's ancestors were making paper about 200 years before that.

Project

Handmade Paper

If you've never made paper before, you may need to prepare yourself for the experience. To do this, make yourself a paper milk shake. Tear one whole sheet of newspaper into small pieces and put them in a blender. Fill the blender with enough water to cover the bits of paper. Blend for a few seconds. Drain as much water as possible from the paper. Spread the pulp out on a piece of canvas or other absorbent fabric and let it dry. This will take the mystery out of the preparation and the process.

Materials

The paper-making sets that are used in this introduction are made from simple, inexpensive materials. Once the sets have been gathered, they may be reused any time. This process is habit-forming!

• paper pulp

The Paper Pulp

Most paper scraps can be used to make pulp. Experiment with a variety of paper such as newsprint, writing paper, paper towels, or construction paper. Colored paper makes colored pulp. Brown paper bags or heavily coated magazine covers should not be used. They do not break up properly.

From *Art Connections*, published by GoodYearBooks. Copyright © 1995 Kimberly Boehler Thompson and Diana Standing Loftus.

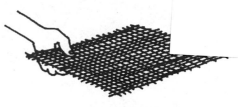

- screen - The best screen for this technique is a needlepoint material called plastic canvas. It is stiff, durable, and will not rust. (It can be found in most hobby supply stores.) Use scissors to cut the screen into 6" x 8" sections or the same size as the paper that is desired. One section is needed for each set.

- blotting cloths–Blotting cloths are pieces of scrap canvas, old blankets, denim, or other absorbant material cut the same size as, or slightly larger than, the screen. Two cloths are needed to handle each sheet of damp paper. They may be reused when dry.

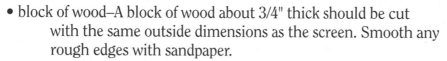

- block of wood–A block of wood about 3/4" thick should be cut with the same outside dimensions as the screen. Smooth any rough edges with sandpaper.

- water pan or tray–A water pan at least 1" deep is needed for each set. This can be a thin aluminum cake pan or any tray that can hold a little water. It must be large enough to set the block of wood inside.

- dowel or rolling pin–A rolling pin (1" or larger diameter) is needed to press water out of the paper pulp. This can be made from a dowel. Cut the dowel to any length that is comfortable to handle (probably about 8").

Ten complete paper-making sets can be used by about 24 students. If the class is going to share the materials, extra blotting cloth should be cut. Two pieces are needed to make each sheet of paper.

Preparation

STEP 1.

Fill a blender half full with scrap paper. (Each scrap should be about 2" square.) Add warm water to the top. Blend on high speed until the bits of paper start to break up into separate fibers. (The amount of water does not matter. It will all be drained from the pulp.) A quart of pulp will make approximately 5 sheets of 6" x 8" paper. Any quantity can be made a day in advance.

STEP 2.

Spread a layer of newspaper over the work surface. Now the class is ready to begin.

Procedure

STEP 1.

Place the block of wood in the empty water tray. Cover the top surface of the wood with one blotting cloth. Set the screen on top of that. The edges of the screen and cloth should line up fairly even with the edges of the wood.

STEP 2.

Pour enough pulp onto the screen to spread a loose, 1/4" thick layer evenly over the area. Smooth this as much as possible with the fingers. Excess water will run into the tray. The water level should always be lower than the top of the wood. If too much water accumulates, set the block aside and empty the tray into a bucket for disposal.

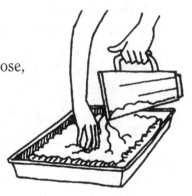

STEP 3.

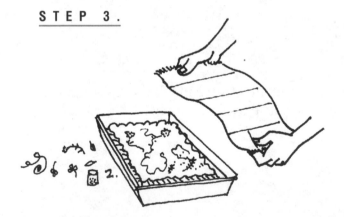

A variety of materials can be arranged on the surface of the pulp at this time to create paper with special effects. Suggestions for materials to use are: dried flowers, magazine picture segments, yarn or thread, colored paper clippings, glitter, drops of food coloring, and different colored pulp.

STEP 4.

Cover the smooth layer of pulp with the other blotting cloth. Roll the dowel or rolling pin over the cloth several times to force the water out of the pulp and into the tray. Keep the screen and pulp layered between the two

From *Art Connections*, published by GoodYearBooks. Copyright © 1995 Kimberly Boehler Thompson and Diana Standing Loftus.

cloths while you lift the layers carefully from the block of wood and lay them pulp-side-down onto several sheets of newspaper.

STEP 5.

Roll the dowel over the layers once again, pressing out as much water as possible. Replace the wet newspapers with dry ones when necessary. With the paper laying face-down, remove the back cloth and gently lift the screen from the pulp. Cover the damp paper again so it is sandwiched between the two cloths. Move it to a table covered with newspaper to dry.

STEP 6.

The top cloth can be removed, allowing the sun or air to dry the paper. (The bottom cloth will support the paper while it's drying and help keep it clean.) It is also possible to speed the drying time by ironing the outside of the cloth for a few minutes before the paper is uncovered. (Be sure the plastic screen has been taken out before ironing.) Dry sheets can be pressed flat overnight under a stack of books or bricks.

The finished sheet of paper will have edges that are feathered instead of straight, like machine-made paper. This uneven quality is called a *deckle edge*. It is the prized identifying mark of handmade paper.

Integrating Ideas

ou have now learned one paper-making process. The correlation between paper making and recycling and its importance can be explained by considering the following:

- Brainstorm all the different kinds of materials people get from trees. Focus on paper and paper products.

- Did you know?

  - The average American uses almost 700 pounds of paper a year.
  - Under ideal growing conditions (the amount of moisture, sunlight, and density of trees), it would take approximately 60 years for a Douglas fir to become a tree 16" in diameter.
  - A 16" diameter tree can contain four 16 foot logs, which can be manufactured into 500 pounds of paper.
  - Two pounds of wood are needed to make one pound of paper.
    (These facts are based on information from the *Forestry Education Unit* developed by Oregon State University and by the U.S. Forest Service.)

- At the end of each day, weigh the paper thrown in the trash. Use the data above to figure the number of trees used to make the paper being thrown away in a week; a month.

- Discuss ways individuals and communities can conserve trees. Locate recycling centers. Find products at home that are packaged in recycled paper.

- If possible, visit a pulp or plywood mill. Write letters or invite guest speakers to talk about conservation and/or recycling. Contact groups such as the U.S. Forest Service, the Audubon Society, National Wildlife Federation, Sierra Club, Friends of the Earth, or a local timber industry spokesperson.

- Research and debate topics related to the tropical rain forest in Brazil and the spotted owl in the Pacific Northwest.

Books

For Teachers and Parents

Lesson Plan Units for Forestry Education. Oregon State University, 1982.

Ranger Rick's Naturescope: Trees Are Terrific. National Wildlife Federation, 1988.

Toale, Bernard. *The Art of Papermaking.* Davis Publications, Inc., 1983.

For Students

Cherry, Lynne. *The Great Kapok Tree.* Harcourt Brace Jovanovich, 1990.

Donahue, Michael. *The Grandpa Tree.* Rinehart Inc., 1988.

Dr. Seuss. *The Lorax.* Random House, 1971.

Gile, John. *The First Forest.* J. Gile Communications, 1989.

Giono, Jean. *The Man Who Planted Trees.* Chelsea Green Pub. Co., 1985

Hindley, Judy. *The Tree.* Crown. Random House, 1990.

Hirschi, Ron. *Discover My World Forest.* A Bantam Little Rooster Book, 1991.

Jaspersohn, William. *How The Forest Grew.* Mulberry Books, 1980.

Romanova, Natalia. *Once There Was a Tree.* Dial Junior Books, 1989.

Wirth, Victoria. *Whisper from the Woods.* Green Tiger Press. Simon & Schuster, 1991.

Printmaking

Leaf a Good Impression

> *"I go to nature to be soothed and healed, and to have my senses put in tune once more."*
>
> *John Burroughs, American writer, 1839–1906*

The Art of Seeing with Relief Prints of Leaves

O riginal prints are classified by the method used to create them. There are four methods of print classification: intaglio, stencil, planographic, and relief. The last method, relief print, is the one used in this lesson.

A Little History

T he relief print was probably the first method to evolve in printmaking history. The oldest relief form is the woodcut, used in ancient China to print religious illustrations. In the western world, the woodblock emerged as a means of printing textiles. Then, in the 15th century, paper mills were established in Europe and the printing press was perfected. This led to the highly developed woodblock technique used to illustrate the earliest books. The woodcut is no longer used in commercial printing, but it is an expressive technique still used by some artists.

Project

Relief Printing

A relief print is made using ink or paint on the raised areas of the printing surface. When the print is made with assorted materials like leaves, string, and cut-out cardboard shapes, it can also be called a *collagraph* because the printing surface resembles a collage. The following activity is an example of this.

Materials

- fresh leaves, flowers, stems, pine branches and other plant materials that can be pressed flat.
- large drawing paper
- paintbrushes about 1/2" wide or soft rubber brayers
- tempera paints plus a small amount of liquid soap
- wooden spoons or other barens
- spray bottle with water
- stack of newspapers
- paint smocks
- Optional printmaking equipment–Brayers and barens are traditional relief printing tools. They are not required to make a relief print, but students enjoy using more professional tools when they are made available. The drying line included in the Preparation stage of this project is a common item used in classrooms and studios for drying prints.

The Brayer

A printmaker will often use a brayer instead of a brush to apply pigment to the relief surface. A good student-grade brayer will have a soft rubber roller (available in a variety of widths). Use it to roll out a sticky layer of paint or waterbase printing ink on a sheet of acrylic or glass (8" x 12" or larger). When the brayer is evenly coated, roll the paint onto the printing surface. Repeat this process several times until a generous coat of paint remains. The printing results will be crisper with this technique.

The Baren

The baren is used to rub (burnish) the back of a print and transfer the pigment (and the impression) onto paper. In relief printing, this tool can be used instead of a printing press. Barens can be purchased in art supply stores. However, a common, inexpensive substitute is the smooth round bottom of a wooden spoon.

The Drying Line

Those who regularly teach in a room the size of a gymnasium won't need a drying line. Others will wonder how they survived printing or painting without one.

Preparation

STEP 1.

Begin with a clothesline that is about 2 feet longer than the distance between the two walls where you are going to hang the line.

STEP 2.

Decide on the number of hangers (clothespins) that you want on the line. Drill a hole about 1/2" down from the top on the front and back of each wooden clothespin. Plastic clothespins can be purchased with the hole already made.

STEP 3.

Leave a 12" length on one end of the clothesline and make a knot. String all of the clothespins through both holes then knot the other end, again leaving about 12" of line.

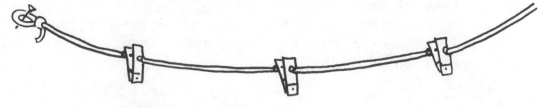

When installing the drying line, keep in mind that the clothespins must be within reach of those who use it. The line can be hung permanently or the ends can be adapted to hang from wall hooks only when needed. Suspend each print from one clothespin to dry.

Procedure

STEP 1.

Choose any combination of sturdy plant materials and arrange them on a few layers of newspaper. (Be sure the plant selection is fresh and not too brittle.)

STEP 2.

Determine which side of the plant to print. (The small veins on the back of a leaf will print a more interesting impression than the front side.) Lay the plant on the newspaper with the side you chose facing up. Mix one teaspoon of liquid soap with about 8 oz of tempera paint. Carefully brush an even coat of paint on the face of the plant. Different colors may be used on different sections to produce a multicolor print.

If using a brayer, spread a small amount of paint mixture (about one tablespoon at first) on a sheet of acrylic or glass. Roll in one direction to coat the roller with paint, then apply the paint to the plant materials. Repeat until the plant materials are evenly covered.

For the best results, just before printing, be sure the paint in all areas has remained wet. If the paint is beginning to dry, moisten the surface using a spray water bottle. (The soap that was added to the paint will slow the drying process.)

STEP 3.

Hold the large sheet of drawing paper over the painted leaves and branches and decide on the best position before laying it down. Once the paper is in place, continue holding it with one hand to prevent movement which can smear the print. (Some movement and smearing may be unavoidable, and may even be desirable.)

STEP 4.

Using care, firmly rub the back of the drawing paper with the bottom of the bowl of a wooden spoon or another baren. When all areas covering the plant materials have been rubbed, lift the print and set it aside to dry. Note that the hard wooden surface used for rubbing will pick up an impression that shows some of the leaf structure and texture. When rubbing is done with the hands, the soft skin pads press the paper into the recessed areas of the leaf and much of the detail is lost. However, with some plant materials this may be necessary for control, and the results will still be pleasing.

Look at the position of the materials on the newspaper. Notice the print is the reverse image. A relief print is always the mirror image of the printing surface.

When the prints are dry, they can be trimmed and mounted on black or colored paper using a glue stick. This very simple way of presenting work creates a finished appearance and gives new artists the opportunity for a fresh look at the beauty in what they've created.

Veggie Prints

Students can also make relief prints with fruits and vegetables. Cut onions, apples, oranges, etc. in half to expose the interesting patterns within. Put a small amount of tempera paint in saucers. Dip the printing surface lightly in the paint. Stamp the impression on a large sheet of paper.

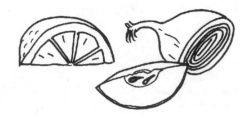

Integrating Ideas

he design made by the veins in a leaf calls attention to the leaf structure. The leaves gathered for printmaking may also be used for the following activities:

- Have students classify the leaves in as many different ways as possible. Categories might include vein structure, color, and shape. Observe the differences and similarities of the leaves in each category.

- Consider whether or not it hurts a plant to remove its leaves. Do plants have feelings? Research and devise experiments to test your theories.

- See the film *The Plant,* in which, without narration, a plant acquires human qualities and takes over its owner's apartment. Also check the category "Books" at the end of this lesson. Nancy McArthur's book *The Plant That Ate Dirty Socks* is an amusing children's book similar in theme.

Books

For Teachers and Parents

Hunken, Jorie, et al. *Botany for All Ages*: *Discovering Nature Through Activities Using Plants.* The Globe Pequot Press, 1989.

Jaffe, Roberta, and Appel, Gary. *The Growing Classroom. Garden Based Science.* Addison-Wesley Publications, 1990.

For Students

Bjork, Christina, and Anderson, Lena. *Linnea's Windowsill Garden.* Raben & Sjogren Publishers. Stockholm, Sweden, 1988.

Carle, Eric. *The Tiny Seed.* Picture Book Studio, 1987.

Heller, Ruth. *Plants That Never Ever Bloom.* Grosset & Dunlap, 1984.

McArthur, Nancy. *The Plant That Ate Dirty Socks.* Avon Books, 1988.

Overbeck, Cynthia. *How Seeds Travel.* Lerner Publishing Co., 1982.

Letter Graphics

Alphabet Antics

> *"Language is the archives of history. . . Language is fossil poetry."*
>
> *Ralph Waldo Emerson 1803–1882, American poet, essayist, and philosopher*

Finding Ways to Discover and Elaborate on the Alphabet

In this lesson, students combine business with pleasure when they design a logo for an imaginary business.

A Little History

The alphabet began thousands of years ago with a need to put ideas into recorded form. In order to describe an event, early humans drew pictures, usually on the walls of caves. From this, the idea of having a picture stand for a word developed. The alphabetic evolution continued, leading to a symbol standing for a sound. Many cultures contributed to this process. Our own English alphabet derives its name from the first two letters of the Greek alphabet, Alpha and Beta.

Designing Logos

An imaginary business needs a logo. This lesson provides students with the opportunity to write interview questions, learn about the occupation of a graphic artist, and become observers and creators of different types of lettering and designs.

Materials

- books from the library with different styles of lettering (Alphabet books are a good source.)
- magazines
- newspapers
- construction paper
- pencils
- marking pens
- crayons
- scissors
- glue
- graph paper
- an overhead made by photocopying various logos from the phone book

Procedure

S T E P 1 .

Help students become familiar with the role of a graphic artist. A graphic artist is the art director, and may do most or all of the design work required on a project. He or she may also coordinate the services of a typographer, calligrapher, or fine artist to satisfy the needs of the customer. The creative process involved in designing a logo begins with an interview. Ideas suggested by the client are incorporated into the final design.

S T E P 2 .

Browse through library books together, taking note of the various type styles. Next glance through newspapers and magazines, cutting out favorite letter styles and words to be arranged into a collage. (See Collage pp. 48-54.)

From *Art Connections*, published by GoodYearBooks. Copyright © 1995 Kimberly Boehler Thompson and Diana Standing Loftus.

STEP 3.

Discuss the meaning of the term *logo*. Help students realize that the lettering and design of a logo can influence potential customers. Use the overhead to show and discuss what logos are, and to look at various lettering styles and designs.

STEP 4.

Have the class work in groups to create a business. Each group will decide the name of the business, products the business sells, and its target market. Then have them try to think of ideas to include in a logo that would symbolize to the public what the business is about and what it does.

STEP 5.

Have students assume the role of graphic artists. Imagine that a representative from a local business has made an appointment with them. Have students compile a list of questions to ask the business representative that would help them plan the concept and design the logo for that company. Sometimes the customer has specific ideas and other times the graphic artist is given freedom to make most of the decisions.

STEP 6.

Have one group act as employees of the business and another group act as the graphic artists. After the graphic artists have asked all of their questions, have the groups switch roles.

STEP 7.

Once the interviews have been conducted and each student has the information needed, he or she can begin the major task of designing logos. At this point, each student will assume the role of a graphic artist. As a graphic artist, he or she will create his or her own lettering. Have students utilize the following steps when working toward a finished product:

a) **Plan**–Spend time looking in books, magazines, and newspapers for ideas. Create thumbnail sketches. These small, rough sketches can encourage students to consider many different options.

b) **Visualize**–What will the final logo look like?

c) **Polish**–Use grid paper to do the final lettering by hand. This will help students get the right proportions. Then have them trace the final letters onto desired paper. Transfers can also be done with carbon paper or by holding the work up to a window. The name of the company should be clearly legible. The design should not distract from the name. (Students can also use various computer programs to design letters.)

From *Art Connections*, published by GoodYearBooks. Copyright © 1995 Kimberly Boehler Thompson and Diana Standing Loftus.

> *"Designing is not a private or solitary activity, it is the resolving of visual problems for specific needs and, more likely, commercial demands."*
>
> *Bruce Robertson*

Integrating Ideas

- Discuss how letters originated.

- Invite students to share their ideas on how they think the first alphabet began. Show examples of alphabets from around the world. *People* by Peter Spier and Volume 1 of an encyclopedia (topic: Alphabet) will have good examples. Do some comparing of letters. Which are favorites?

- Investigate other forms of communication such as Braille and sign language.

- Beatrix Potter is best known for her wonderfully written and illustrated children's books. But she was also the creator of her own alphabet. From the ages of 14–30, she wrote in a journal using a secret code. "It took Leslie Linder and a part-time cryptographer six years to break the code, and another eight to translate the whole text and get *The Journal of Beatrix Potter* into print," writes Timothy Foote in a *Smithsonian* article. Have students try creating and breaking each other's secret codes.

Books

For Teachers and Parents

Anderson, Charles R. *Letter Graphics*. Van Nostrand Reinhold Company, 1982.

Blankholm, Robert F. *Twenty-Six Friends*. Stagecoach Road Press, 1990.

Jean, Georges. *Writing, The Story of Alphabets and Scripts*. Harry N. Abrams, Inc., 1987.

Robertson, Bruce. *Designing with Letters*. Watson-Guptill Publications, 1988.

Zaslow, David. *What's in a Word*. Good Apple, Inc., 1983.

For Students

Base, Graeme. *Animalia.* Harry N. Abrams, Inc., 1986.

Burton, Albert, Jr. *Top Secret! Codes to Crack.* Albert Whitman & Co., 1987.

MacDonald, Suse. *Alphabatics.* Bradbury Press, 1986.

Roehrig, Catharine. *Fun with Hieroglyphs.* Metropolitan Museum of Art. Viking, 1990.

Spier, Peter. *People.* Doubleday, 1980.

Tatchell, Judy, and Varley, Carol. *How to Draw Lettering.* Usborne Publishing LTD. London, 1991.

Van Allsburg, Chris. *The Z Was Zapped: A Play in Twenty-Six Acts.* Houghton Mifflin Co., 1987.

Mail Art

Inspiring Letter Writing

Using Mail Art as a Motivator

Using ideas from this lesson can make letter writing an exciting activity. Activities for making stationery, greeting cards, stamps, and envelopes are all included in the following pages. This lesson also incorporates establishing and running a school-wide post office.

A Little History

After World War II, many American artists began to question the role and meaning of art in modern society. Many decided that the art "idea" was more important than the art object. These beliefs led to the Conceptual Art movement of the 70s. Conceptual artists rebelled against traditional art forms and searched for alternative methods of presenting their ideas. For some, Mail Art became their medium and the mailbox their gallery.

From *Art Connections*, published by GoodYearBooks. Copyright © 1995 Kimberly Boehler Thompson and Diana Standing Loftus.

Today, art schools and organizations all over the world request submissions based on a theme for Mail Art exhibitions. It is an opportunity for persons of all ages to submit artwork in a variety of media and have it exhibited. To find mail art announcements, look in the classified or competitions section of art publications such as *ARTWEEK*. (West Coast, Oakland)

Projects

 he next few pages include an all-occasion assortment of ideas and instructions for greeting cards, envelopes, stickers, stamps, and stationery.

Pop-up Cards

Cards can be made from Collage techniques (pp. 48-54), using handmade paper (page 75), or Letter Graphics (pp. 88-93). Designs for the cards can be created using stamps and stickers described in this section. Following are basic instructions for making pop-up cards. Any of these ideas can be combined to create a greeting with an original message.

Materials

- white or colored paper or cardstock approx. 8 1/2" x 11"
- glue stick or paste
- scissors
- colored pencils, pens, or crayons

Two pieces of paper the same size are needed for one pop-up card. Cardstock, a heavier grade of paper available in print shops or stationery stores, is an optional material for a finer quality card.

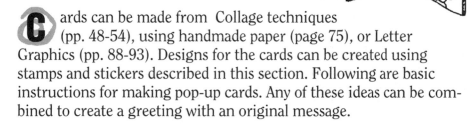

Procedure

STEP 1.

Fold both sheets in half top to bottom. One piece will have the pop-up section cut into it, the other will be the backing and the cover.

STEP 2.

On one piece of paper, cut 2 parallel lines in from the fold. The size and location of the cuts determine the size and location of the pop-up section.

STEP 3.

Fold the cut strip back and then out again. Open the paper and crease the pop-up strip in the opposite direction.

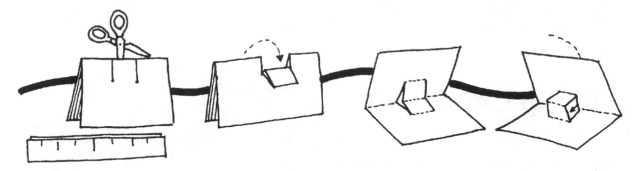

STEP 4.

Decide what the pop-up figure will be. Draw, color, and cut the figure out. Paste this to the front of the pop-up strip, while holding the card at a 45° angle.

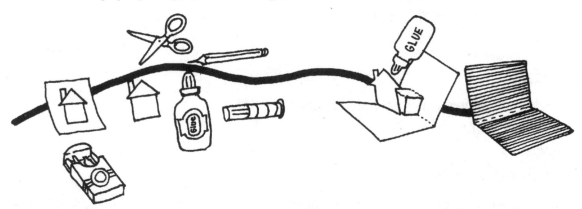

STEP 5.

Fold the card in half again with the pop-up section to the inside, and paste it to the inside of the other folded sheet. Keep paste on the outside edges and away from the pop-up strip.

Different-sized and shaped sections can be cut to pop-up together. Experiment and construct inventions of your own.

Stickers

Materials

- paper
- sticker paste
- 3/4" or 1" brush
- pencil
- colored pens
- scissors

Procedure

Brush a thin coat of sticker paste on one side of a sheet of paper. Let paste dry, then turn the paper over to draw and color the sticker or label designs. (They can be any size.) When finished, cut stickers out, moisten, and apply to paper or cardboard surfaces.

Sticker Paste Recipe

- four 1 ounce packets unflavored gelatin
- 6 Tablespoons white vinegar
- 1 Tablespoon pure lemon extract

S T E P   1 .

Bring vinegar to a boil. Remove from heat and stir in gelatin until completely dissolved. Add extract and mix well.

S T E P   2 .

Store paste in a glass jar. When cooled, it will become a gel. This can be stored for several months. To reuse, set the jar in a pan of boiling water until paste is liquid again.

Rubber Stamps

Materials

- pencil or pen
- gum eraser found in office or art supply stores (these are soft and easy to carve)
- carving tool (We suggest a serrated steak knife for younger students; older students may use an exacto knife or linoleum gouge.)

Procedure

STEP 1.

Invite students to decide on the image that they want to print. Tell them to keep the idea simple.

STEP 2.

Have them sketch the shape onto any side of the eraser.

STEP 3.

Tell them to use a pen to darken the area that they plan to leave uncarved. (The uncarved portion of the surface leaves the imprint.) Remember that the stamp will print a reverse image. Certain symbols (letters, words, flags) have a correct direction. These should be drawn and carved backwards. Tell them that they can check the sketch in front of a mirror.

STEP 4.

The surface of the eraser can be safely carved with a serrated steak knife. Small groups of 5th or 6th grade students may use an exacto knife or linoleum gouge with a narrow blade to carve a

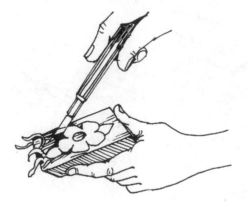

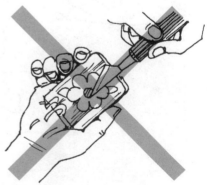

crisper image. Constant supervision is necessary when instructing beginners. The eraser should always be held to the side of the line being cut. **Knives may slip in the direction of the pressure. Keep fingers out of the path.**

STEP 5.

As much as possible, make cuts that are a V or U shape. Undercutting the raised surface of the stamp can cause a portion of it to break off. The depth of the cuts should be about 1/16th to 1/8th of an inch.

STEP 6.

Use the stamp pad to moisten the carved surface of the rubber stamp. Stamps can be placed on any smooth, flat surface.

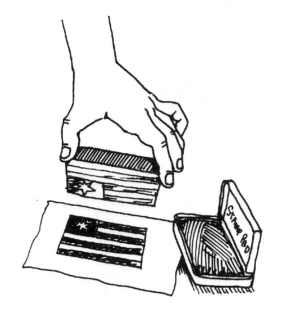

Stamp Pad

Materials

- piece of felt at least 1/4" thick
- tempera paint
- spray bottle with water

Procedure

STEP 1.

Dampen a piece of felt with tempera paint.

STEP 2.

Felt pads may be placed in shallow plastic containers to be reused. The pad can be kept moist by spraying lightly with water. These pads are ideal for classroom use, but the prints are not waterproof. For more permanent results, use a commercial ink pad.

Stationery

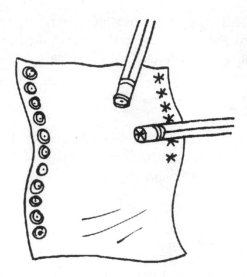

Use a single rubber stamp or a combination of them to decorate cards, envelopes, packages, and of course, stationery. For variation, try different colors and repeat or overlap the design.

Envelopes

STEP 1.

Select an interesting sheet of paper such as a magazine page or gift wrap. It should be at least 8 1/2" x 11".

STEP 2.

Photocopy page 101 to use as a pattern. The envelope pattern included here is for a 3 1/2" x 4 1/2" envelope, but can be enlarged to a standard size. Cut the envelope shape out of the paper you've chosen.

STEP 3.

With the right side of the envelope facing down, fold flaps A and B back as shown by the dotted line.

STEP 4.

Glue the areas of flaps A and B as shown. Fold C down on top to fasten. Leave the top flap open until it's time to seal the envelope.

STEP 5.

The sticker paste recipe included in this lesson can be used instead of glue to fasten all the flaps, including the top.

From *Art Connections*, published by GoodYearBooks. Copyright © 1995 Kimberly Boehler Thompson and Diana Standing Loftus.

(R E P R O D U C I B L E   P A G E)

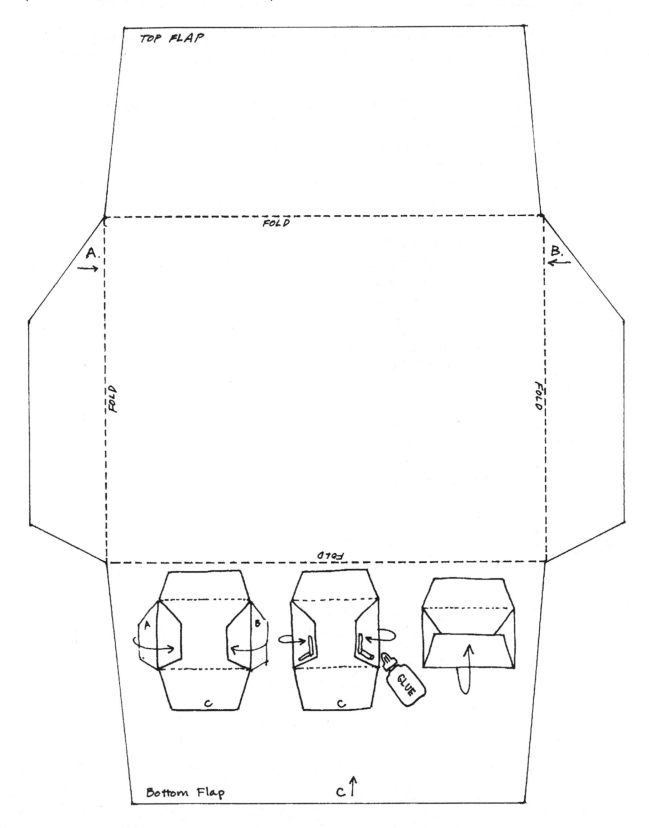

TOP FLAP

FOLD

A.

B.

FOLD

FOLD

FOLD

A

B

C

C

GLUE

Bottom Flap

C

Integrating Ideas

The preceding activities can be used to make letter writing more interesting and fun. The following ideas can add to this excitement and give insights into the operation of a real post office.

- Use the books *Messages in the Mailbox* and *The Jolly Postman* to add interest in and a sense of fun to letter writing.

- Create a school-wide post office. Decide on a workable length of time for the post office to be in operation. In the beginning, it may be desirable to keep the duration short (around 2 weeks). As a class, brainstorm options for creating a post office. Use refrigerator boxes, several smaller boxes, desks, tables, butcher paper, paint, and so forth. Have stamp pads available at the post office and in each classroom.

- Conduct a classroom or school-wide contest to design stamps. Photocopy pages of the winning stamp design to be given to teachers. Use sticker paste to adhere stamps to letters. Decide on street names. Make mailboxes out of shoeboxes labelled with the new addresses. Give teachers a list of the addresses to post in their rooms.

- Organize a field trip to a post office.

- Invite a letter carrier as a guest speaker. What are the various jobs that take place in a real post office? How are these similar or different from the needs of the school post office?

- Extend letter writing to other subject areas. Make cards or stationery using a theme. Following historical research of colonial times, imagine that you live in a southern colony and write to a friend telling about a typical day. Pretend to be a character in a book. Write a letter to another character. Write a letter to the editor regarding social issues such as the tropical rain forest or endangered animals.

Books

For Teachers and Parents

Chatani, M. *Pop-Up Greeting Cards*. Ondorisha Publishers, LTD.

P.S. Write Soon. U.S. Postal Service and National Council of Teachers of English, 1982.

For Students

"Mail Art." *Kids Art News,* issue 13 (Spring, 1989).

Ahlberg, Janet, and Ahlberg, Allan. *The Jolly Postman.* Little Brown & Co., 1986.

Cleary, Beverly. *Dear Mr. Henshaw.* Dell Publishing Co., 1983

DePaola, Tomie. *What the Mailman Brought.* Putnam Publishers, 1987.

Leedy, Loreen. *Messages in the Mailbox, How to Write a Letter.* Holiday House, 1991.

Potter, Beatrix. *Yours Affectionately, Peter Rabbit.* Frederick Warne Publishers Ltd., London, 1983.

Williams, Jennifer. *Stringbean's Trip to the Shining Sea.* Scholastic Inc., 1990.

Bookmaking

> *"You can't wait for inspiration. You have to go after it with a club."*
>
> *Jack London,*
> *American writer,*
> *1876–1916*

Finishing Touches

Binding a book is like framing a painting. The various elements should work together and appear as one finished piece. Various imaginative bookmaking options are included in this lesson. Students combine their favorite piece of writing with a chosen bookmaking technique. Ideas for celebrating and publishing their efforts are included.

A Little History

One art movement of the 20th century centered around the book as an art form. This movement's popularity began early in the century as an alternative way for artists to spread their views. Many artists experimented with the medium. Some believed that this new format was well-suited for what they wanted to express. The introduction of photocopying led to the artist's book movement of the 70s. Since that time, artists have playfully explored the possibilities of the medium. Some books are narratives, others are toys, and some become works of sculpture.

The cover, pages, size, shape, and color of a book all contribute to the total enjoyment of a story. Cover designs and page illustrations can be developed with Collage techniques (pp. 48-54), Cartoon Drawing (pp. 68-74), or rubber stamps (pp. 98-99). Pop-up books can be created with the pop-up card instructions found in the Mail Art lesson.

Hand-Sewn Book

This method of binding produces a versatile book with a nice finish. It is ideal for a journal, scrapbook, or original story. These instructions are for a 9" x 12" book with 6 leaves (12 pages) and a paper cover. The process is the same for any size book.

Book size can be adjusted using a **template.** The template is made from a strip of cardboard or tagboard, 2" wide and 12" long. Place a ruler along the edge of the strip. Starting 2" down from the top, make 5 marks that are 2" apart. Use scissors to cut a small ^ out of the edge at each mark. (The template for any other size book should be the length of the folded edge with 5 evenly spaced notches.)

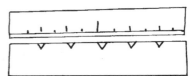

Materials

- 6 sheets of 18" x 12" white paper
- 1 colored sheet–18" x 12"
- 1 yard of colored thread
- 1 large needle
- 1 cardboard template to mark the position of holes for sewing the pages together

The Fundamentals of Folding

Attractive books often depend on accurate folds. Here are two terms used in the art of folding. Students can use them to impress their friends.

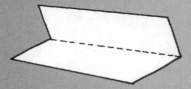
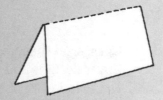

The Hot Dog Fold—Fold in half, from side to side (or lengthwise).

The Hamburger Fold—Fold in half, top to bottom.

To make a correct fold, bend the paper into position and hold the edges together with one hand. With the other hand, smooth the paper down the center to the fold and crease outward, first on one side, then on the other.

Procedure

STEP 1.

Fold the 7 sheets of paper in half, one at a time using the hamburger fold. Stack the folded sheets one on top of the other. Fasten the stack securely at the fold with a few paper clips.

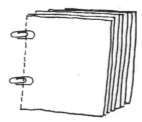

STEP 2.

Lay the template along the outside folded edge of the stack. Draw the ^ in all 5 positions. The marks should appear evenly spaced and centered. Hold the pages in place and cut the ^ shape out at the fold. Now put the pages one inside of the other with the cover on the outside.

STEP 3.

Thread the needle with yarn. Open the book and lace it together as follows: letter each hole from the bottom, A, B, C, D, E. Pull the yarn down through hole A. Leave a loose end about 6" long. Then weave the other end of the yarn up into B, down into C, up into D, down into E, around the edge and down into E, up into D, down into C, up into B, and down into A. Tie both ends around the edge in a knot or bow.

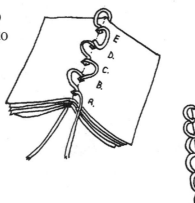

A Book with a Different Shape

he shape of a book can be determined by the main subject or character in a story.

Procedure

STEP 1.

Draw a pattern.

STEP 2.

Lay the pattern on two sheets of colored paper, fasten in several places with paper clips, and cut the outline with sharp scissors. This is the front and back cover.

STEP 3.

Use the same pattern to cut the pages.

STEP 4.

Punch holes and join the pages together with yarn, pipe cleaners, or book rings found in office supply stores. This is the easiest and best binding to use with this type of book. If you prefer to staple the pages, a piece of colored cloth tape will hide the staple and leave an attractive edge.

Folded Book

ny single sheet of paper can be converted into a compact, 6-page book.

Procedure

STEP 1.

Fold paper in half using a hamburger fold.

STEP 2.

Unfold the paper and fold in half again; this time make a hot dog fold. (The folded paper now has a crease across the center.)

STEP 3.

Fold both ends of the folded paper to the center crease. This will divide the sheet into 8 equal rectangles.

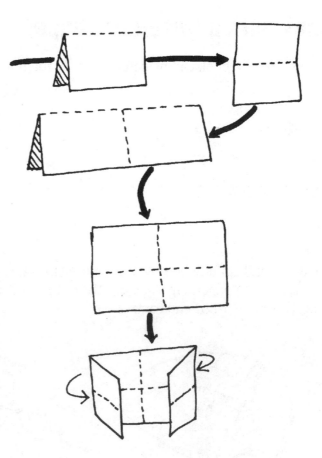

STEP 4.

Unfold the paper and cut a line on the center crease from point A to point B as shown.

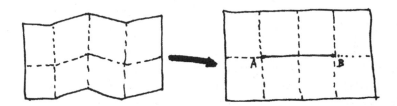

STEP 5.

Return paper to the hot dog fold position with the partially cut, folded edge facing up. Hold the paper so the cut section forms a diamond shape. Now, following the illustration, identify points A, B, C, and D at the four corners of the diamond opening. Gently separate points C and D while bringing points A and B together. The shape of the top edge will resemble an X.

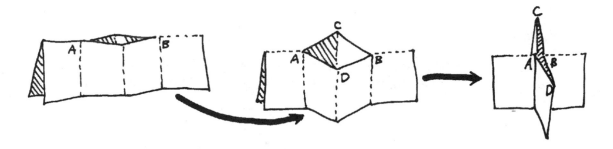

STEP 6.

Now, fold the pages around to form a book. To finish, straighten and crease the folds again.

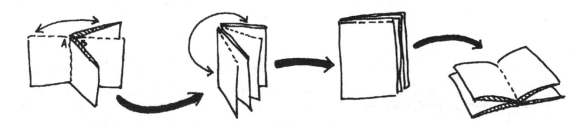

This can be a pocket journal or a picture book. If you open up a finished book, you will see that all the pictures or words appear on just one side of the paper. This makes it possible to plan a story, poem, or list of rules that can be photocopied, then folded and used in class.

Rainbow Book

The shapes and colors that make up this book are a reminder of the beautiful paper cutouts by Henri Matisse (French, twentieth-century artist). Initially the possibilities and the patterns are always a surprise. The design itself may inspire some colorful writing.

Procedure

STEP 1.

Cut colored paper into long rectangular strips. The recommended size is 18" x 6" (1/2 sheet standard size construction paper), but this can vary according to paper availability or your preference.

STEP 2.

Select a color assortment for the pages of the book. Use about 6 pages the first time or a thickness of paper that can comfortably be cut with scissors. Choose one extra, uncut strip to save for the cover.

STEP 3.

Arrange the colors and lay the pages together. Space the ends of the strips in order to expose the different layers. Line up the sides of the paper and secure with paper clips.

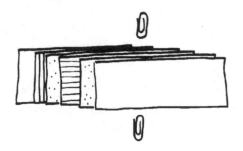

STEP 4.

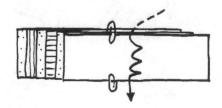

With sharp scissors, cut a wavy pattern across the paper layers, near the center of the strip. There are now two sets of pages to combine or use separately. Both sections have a wavy end and a straight end. Line up the straight edges of each section and see the rainbow pattern appear.

STEP 5.

Place the cover strip underneath the other pages. Let the straight edge extend slightly beyond the wavy pattern at the bottom. Line up all the pages, fold the remaining portion of the cover over the top of the book, and staple along this fold.

Chinese Puzzle Book

Guaranteed to arouse curiosity and interest, it functions well as a question and answer book or a magical alternative to flash cards.

Each book is made with a 9" x 12" sheet of colored paper and 2 paper strips, 2 3/4" x 9", in a contrasting color.

Procedure

STEP 1.

Make the following folds with the larger sheet. Fold in half then in half again using a hotdog fold. Open the sheet of paper. Make a hamburger fold. Keeping the paper folded, fold both ends to the center.

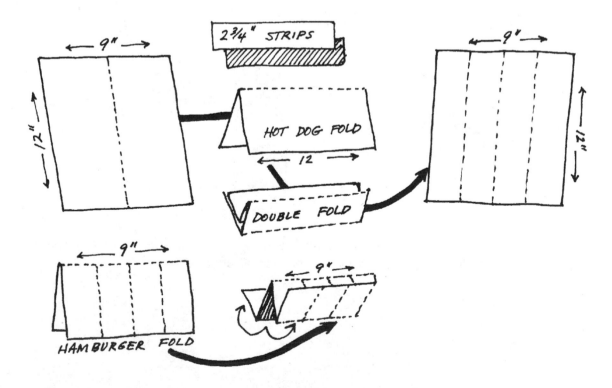

STEP 2.

Unfold the paper. Cut lines AD, BE, and CF as shown.

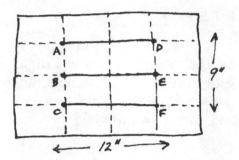

STEP 3.

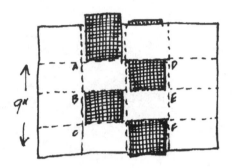

Weave a colored paper strip through the cut lines, and slide it to the left side. Use the other strip to reverse the weave through the remaining cut lines on the right.

STEP 4.

Hold the book so it looks like a "W" from the end. Close it together to pull apart the two hidden pages. Open the book and separate the pages carefully.

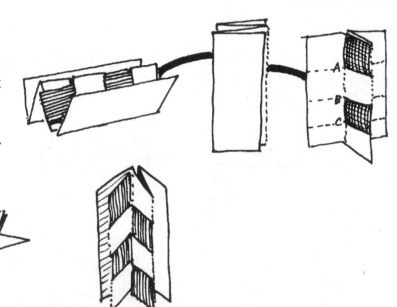

Write questions or riddles in the colored rectangles and put the answers on the secret side. Amazing? Turn the book over to write another set of questions.

From *Art Connections*, published by GoodYearBooks. Copyright © 1995 Kimberly Boehler Thompson and Diana Standing Loftus.

Integrating Ideas

◉ After editing a favorite piece of writing, organize the layout in a dummy book made of stapled newsprint. Arrange words on the pages and note the position and subject of the illustrations. This is a process similar to what published authors do. A title page, table of contents, and a page telling about the author can add a special touch.

◉ A variety of ways to create books are mentioned in this lesson. Transform the plans into a polished product.

◉ When completed, consider the following possibilities: (A) Have a classroom Author's Reception. Invite parents and serve refreshments. (B) Plan a schedule in which students are sent to other classrooms in the school to share their finished books. (C) Have students enter their story in a contest or try to get it published. The magazine *Stone Soup* accepts children's work. Also check the list in this lesson under "Books."

◉ Opportunities to share the joys of writing should be plentiful. Invite an author or newsreporter as a guest. Write with the students and share some of your own writing. Ask students for their feedback. Saturate your classroom in the printed word. Let students see writing as something fun and as an important part of the world, inside and outside the classroom.

Books

For Teachers and Parents

Atwell, Nancie. *In the Middle.* Heinemann, 1987.

Calkins, Lucy McCormick. *Living Between the Lines.* Heinemann, 1991.

Henderson, Kathy. *Market Guide for Young Writers,* rev. ed. Shoe Tree Press, 1990.

Murray, Donald M. *Write to Learn.* Holt Rinehart & Winston, Inc., 1987.

Willis, Meredith Sue. *Personal Fiction Writing.* Teachers & Writer's Collaborative, 1984.

For Students

Aliki. *How a Book Is Made.* Harper & Row, 1986.

Papier-Mâché

> "*Some stories are to be tasted, others to be swallowed and some few to be chewed and digested.*"
>
> *Francis Bacon,*
> *English philosopher*
> *and statesman,*
> *1561–1626*

Using Papier-Mâché to Motivate Writing

Fictional stories, poems, and the thesaurus can be used in this lesson to capture the essence of student's papier-mâché creatures. In describing the creature they make, students will give form to their words. All it takes is a wild imagination, paper, paste, and a little patience.

A Little History

Papier-mâché means mashed paper. The process is similar to paper making, with a paste added to the pulp for strength. Its origins are also similar to paper making. Examples of papier-mâché materials from early Egypt still exist today, and it is believed that it was used in ancient China as well. The French were the first Europeans known to use papier-mâché. Beginning in the 1600s, they made elegant boxes, bowls, and trays.

During the 1800s, the English became noted for furniture produced from the material. Today it is still popular for craftspeople and artists, who use the mixture to create jewelry, masks, toys, and sculpture.

Papier-Mâché Creature

Materials

The papier-mâché framework is called a *form*. The form material examples included below can be crushed or combined and held in place with tape, wire, string, or rubberbands. Tell students that the basic shape can be as big as they dare.

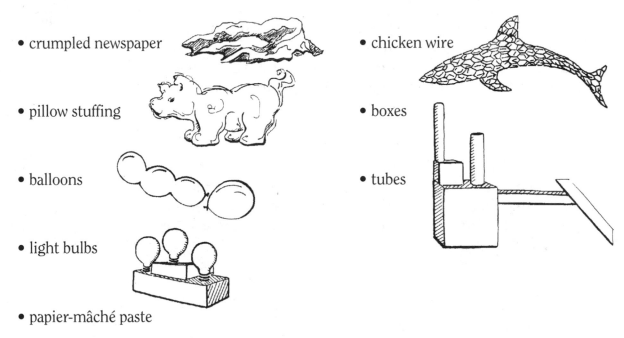

- crumpled newspaper

- pillow stuffing

- balloons

- light bulbs

- papier-mâché paste

- chicken wire

- boxes

- tubes

A removable form can also be used. Grease the object with petroleum jelly and cover it with a layer of wet newspaper or wax paper. This makes it easy to separate the object from the dry papier-mâché shell. Warm soapy water will remove any paste and paper that remains on the form.

Newspaper strips should be torn about 1" wide into lengths. (The torn edge adheres to the shape better than a cut edge.) Before starting the papier-mâché process, fill 2 or 3 large paper bags with enough strips to cover each form with several layers of newspaper.

Papier-mâché paste holds the paper layers together and leaves a stiff, dried shape. Prepare it in a tub or bucket. The paste should be the consistency of buttermilk or gravy. The amount needed will vary, depending on the size of the project and number of students. Begin with at least a gallon of the mixture.

Papier-mâché Paste

- Liquid starch–Use straight from the bottle or slightly diluted with water
- Instant laundry starch–Mix equal parts starch and cold water
- White glue–Dilute 2 parts glue with 1 part water
- Wheat paste or wallpaper paste–Follow directions on the package for a paste the consistency of thick cream

Procedure

STEP 1.

Place the form on a large piece of wax paper with several sheets of newspaper underneath to catch the drips. Dip the newspaper strips, one at a time, into the papier-mâché paste. While holding the strip over the mixture, run it gently between two fingers to remove excess paste. Cover the form so the edges of the paper overlap. Apply several layers in all directions.

STEP 2.

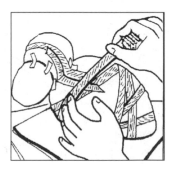

Let the basic shape dry for a few hours or overnight. Add arms, legs, and a tail. These can be made from rolled or wadded form materials. Cover and secure these parts with a few layers of papier-mâché. During this final stage, yarn or fabric can be dipped in paste and applied to the surface for texture.

STEP 3.

The papier-mâché figure should be completely dry in 2 or 3 days. Once it is dry, it is ready to paint. (Tempera is best in the classroom.) When the paint is dry, students may want to glue on eyes, mouth, hair, or clothing using buttons, feathers, felt, or other beautiful scraps.

Integrating Ideas

- When students have finished creating their creatures, have them use their creatures for writing activities.

- Invite students to think of as many words as possible to describe their creature. This might be a good time to tie in a lesson using the thesaurus. It could also be an opportunity for writing some expressive poems.

- Questions to help motivate stories could include: Where does your creature live? Who are its friends? What does it eat? What does it enjoy doing during the day or night? What kinds of problems might it encounter?

Books

For Teachers and Parents

Calkins, Lucy McCormick. *The Art of Teaching Writing*. Heinemann, 1986.

Denman, Gregory A. *When You've Made It Your Own (Teaching Poetry)*. Heinemann, 1988.

Graves, Donald H. *Experiment with Fiction*. Heinemann, 1989.

For Students

Van Allsburg, Chris. *The Mysteries of Harris Burdick*. Houghton Mifflin Co., 1984.

Poetry

Larrick, Nancy, comp. *Cats Are Cats*. Philomel Books, 1988.

Moss, Jeff. *The Butterfly Jar*. Bantam Books, 1989.

Silverstein, Shel. *A Light in the Attic*. Harper & Row, 1974.

———. *Where the Sidewalk Ends*. Harper & Row, 1981.

Sing a Song of Popcorn: Every Child's Book of Poems; selected by Beatrice Schenk de Regniers, Eva Moore, Mary Michaels White, and Jan Car. Scholastic Inc., 1988.

The Random House Book of Poetry; selected by Jack Prelutsky. Random House, 1983.

Felting

Cultural Awareness

> "Art is a universal language and through it each nation makes its own unique contribution to the culture of mankind."
>
> *Dwight D. Eisenhower, U.S. President, 1890–1969*

Linking Felt and China

This soapy, squeezing, hands-on experience gives students the opportunity to learn about feltmaking. It is tied with a cultural look at China, which has a history that includes feltmaking.

A Little History

In the book *Feltmaking: Techniques and Projects,* Inge Evers writes, "Felt was so important in the lives of the Mongols and the people in Chinese and Russian Turkistan that during the Middle Ages the whole northern steppe district was known to the Chinese as 'the land of felt.'"

Wool has the unique characteristic of being able to become bonded, or woven, by using pressure by agitation, some heat, soap, and water. Bonding wool in this way is called *felting*. This process has been used for thousands of years by nomads to make their tents. Other cultures have used the process to make rugs, saddle blankets, mittens, slippers, dolls, and garments.

Felt Balls

Materials

- one-half ounce (per student) of dyed sheep's wool
  or
- one-half ounce of undyed sheep's wool plus one-half of a 32 oz. package of Kool-Aid™ (per student)
- soap flakes or powder
- water
- large containers

Preparation

The following directions will provide two students with dyed wool. Increase according to the number of students in your class. Dissolve one 32 oz package of Kool-Aid™ in 4 cups of cold water. Add 2 half-ounce pieces of wool. Using a long handled utensil, gently push the wool into the Kool-Aid and water dye mixture until it is completely immersed. Do not stir. Let this set for at least two hours. Put the wool on a tray or rack to dry for a couple of days. Do not wring it.

Each student will need a half-ounce piece of dyed wool. Make soapy water in a large container using 1 cup of soap flakes or powder to 1 gallon of hot water. Students will be putting their hands in this water. Keep this in mind when deciding the temperature.

Procedure

STEP 1.

Give each student a half-ounce piece of dyed wool. Have students pull the wool into thin, 2 inch-long pieces, and layer them one on top of the other in opposite directions. When they are finished, have them form their hands around the wool, gently pushing and shaping it into a ball.

STEP 2.

Students should move to assigned areas, bringing the wool with them. Have them immerse their hands in soapy water, then remove their soapy hands from the water and begin to massage the dry wool ball. Slowly immerse the ball into the soapy water. For the next 10 minutes, squeeze and shape the ball constantly in the water.

STEP 3.

Hold the ball just above the water and use the soap bubbles to shape and smooth it. Do this for 5 minutes.

STEP 4.

Rinse with cold water. Set out to dry.

Integrating Ideas

Discover more about China by considering the following:

- Peter Spier's book *People* does an excellent job of developing an appreciation for the differences in people all over the world. It can be enjoyed by any age level.
- Find the connections between China and the following: wheelbarrow, kites, block printing, compass, ink, an abacus, porcelain, and puppets in shadow play.
- Compare China to the United States. Research China's language, schools, money, places of interest, religions, diet, architecture, holidays, politics, arts, and crafts.
- Learn how to use chopsticks, and then have lunch together at a Chinese restaurant. (Be aware of any food allergies.)
- Research, re-create, and celebrate your own Chinese New Year.

Books

For Teachers and Parents

Evers, Inge. *Feltmaking: Techniques and Projects.* Lark Books, 1987.

Freeman, Sue. *Felt Craft.* A David & Charles Craft Book. Sterling Publishing Co., Inc., 1988.

Schuman, Jo Miles. *Art from Many Hands.* Davis Publications, Inc., 1981.

Vickrey, Anne Einset. *Felting by Hand.* Crafts Works Publishing, 1987.

For Students

Blood, Charles L., and Link, Martin. *The Goat in the Rug.* Aladdin Books. Macmillan Publishing Co., 1990.

De Paola, Tomie. *Charlie Needs a Cloak.* Prentice-Hall, Inc., 1973.

Fisher, Leonard E. *The Great Wall of China.* Macmillan Publishing Co., 1986.

Fritz, Jean. *China Homecoming.* Putnam Publishing Co., 1985.

Levinson, Riki. *Our Home Is the Sea.* Dutton Children's Books, 1988.

Louie, Ai-Ling. *Yeh-Shen: A Cinderella Story from China.* Philomel Books, 1982.

Miles, Miska. *Annie and the Old One.* Little Brown & Co., 1971.

Spier, Peter. *People.* Doubleday, 1980.

Tan, Amy. *The Moon Lady.* Macmillan Publishing Co., 1992.

Waters, Kate, and Slovenz-Low, Madeline. *Lion Dancer: Ernie Wan's Chinese New Year.* Penguin USA., 1990.

Yen, Clara. *Why Rat Comes First: The Story of the Chinese Zodiac.* Childrens Book Press, 1991.

Young, Ed. *Lon Po Po.* Philomel. New York. 1990.

Optical Art

Deceptive Geometry

Optical Explanation

In art, geometrical elements such as line, angle, and shape can create illusions. In this lesson, students explore the art and science of optical art and how optical art can "trick" the eye. They examine op art done by artists, learn about the illusion of movement, and create their own illusions.

A Little History

R. L. Gregory, in his essay *The Confounded Eye*, observed that "Scientists fight error, while artists court illusion." The most common experience we have with artistic illusion is to "see" three-dimensional form on a surface we know is flat (two-dimensional). Artists use perspective (depth) to give this three-dimensional illusion. By the height of the Renaissance, this concept of creating perspective was widely understood in the art world.

The knowledge of perspective that made it possible for artists to paint an illusion of the real world inspired others to distort that illusion. The popular graphics of M. C. Escher remind us that we can't always believe our eyes. The bottom strip of this Escher tessellation illustrates how the artist playfully uses perspective.

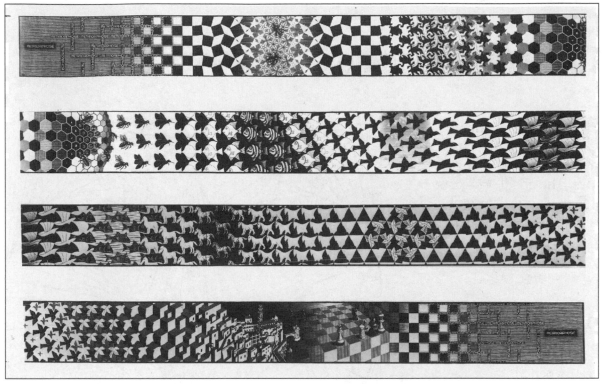

Op Art

In the 60s, an artistic trend appeared which made the world dizzy with a new kind of illusion. This trend was (and still is) known as op art. Artists such as Vasarely, Bridget Riley, and Richard Anuszkiewicz dazzled spectators with the illusion of movement in their calculated paintings.

Op art challenges the eye with the experience of its own visual system. As we scan a piece of op art, the eye will seek a comfortable point of focus. When it is unable to find one, it becomes fatigued. Retinal fatigue causes the after-images

Jean Larcher: *Optical and Geometrical Allover Patterns.* Dover Publications.

that appear constantly when viewing high contrast, repetitive patterns. Rapid eye movement across the pattern increases the confusion and the optical sensation.

The Optical Doodle

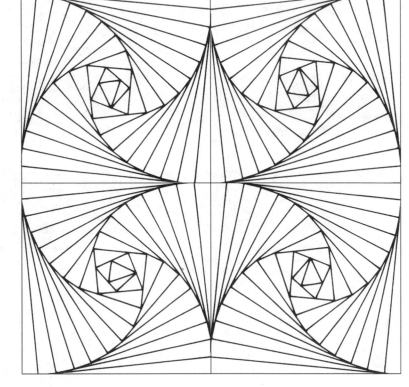

This interesting curved pattern is made using only straight lines. The doodle consists of four identical designs, each constructed separately.

Materials

- white drawing paper
- pencil
- ruler

Procedure

STEP 1.

Draw a 4" square on a piece of paper. With a pencil and a ruler, evenly divide it into four 2" squares. At the top and bottom of the larger square, mark the center point of each line. The drawing in each square starts at these points.

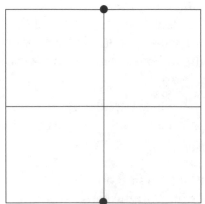

STEP 2.

Begin the design of the lower left square at the bottom starting point. (See illustration.) The drawing can be done freehand or with a ruler. The entire pattern is made from a continuous line moving counterclockwise that repeatedly leaves a narrow wedge shape. Try to keep the wide end of the wedge the same size throughout the design. Follow the illustrated steps, rotating the paper if necessary. Continue drawing until the square is filled and you can go no further.

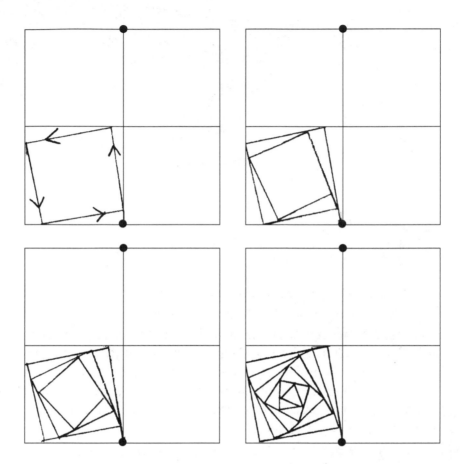

Adaptations of 2 figures on pages 69–70 from EXPERIMENTS IN OPTICAL ILLUSION by Nelson F. Beeler and Franklyn M. Branley. Illustrated by Fred H. Lyon. Copyright 1951 by Thomas Y. Crowell. Reprinted by permission of HarperCollins Publishers, Inc.

STEP 3.

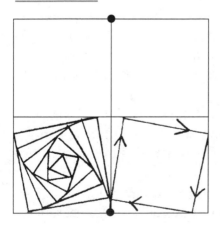

After finishing the first section of the doodle, draw the design in the lower right square, beginning at the same starting point. This time, however, the continuous line is drawn clockwise. To draw the designs in the two squares on top, turn the paper upside-down and proceed as before.

STEP 4.

This activity can be simplified by drawing only a single square or students can elaborate with color and variations of their own.

A variety of tools and materials can be used to inspire original optical designs. Students can experiment with a compass, various templates, or graph paper. Or they can cut and paste shapes from lined wrapping paper for an illusionary collage. Just remember that contrast (light against dark) is a key element in producing optical effects.

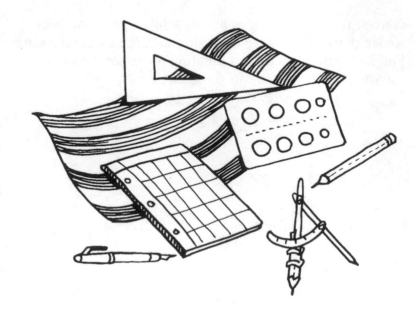

Integrating Ideas

- ❂ While studying geometry, it may be noted that many optical designs use the elements of line, angle, square, circle, and various other shapes.

- ❂ Make an overhead of the reproducible page. Project the page on a screen. Have groups of students study the figures. Each group should then work to reach a consensus for the answers to problems 1–5. Record each group's answers. Discuss what is happening in each figure to create an optical illusion. (The environment can alter the way a shape appears.) Based on this experience, have students write and share their definition of an optical illusion.

- ❂ Apply geometry and symmetry to the study of *tessellations* (puzzlelike designs made popular by M. C. Escher).

- ❂ Students may want to research the work of Ewald Hering, Johannes Peter Müller, or Whilhelm Wundt; all scientists who have done studies on optical illusions.

- ❂ Think about illusions in relation to everyday life. Examples: Occasionally STOP is painted directly on the street before an intersection as a signal to drivers. Why are letters painted in the elongated (distorted) form? Why is the word AMBULANCE printed backward on the front of this emergency vehicle?

- ❂ Nature has many illusions such as camouflage, the rising and setting of the sun, a mirage of water in the desert, and the size of a full moon over the mountains compared to a full moon in the sky. Invite students to think of other illusions created by nature.

- ❂ Packaging, size, line, and color are used to sell a product. In fashion, color, shoulder pads, stripes, makeup, and pocket placement can flatter or detract from appearance. Look for illusions in advertisements.

- ❂ Research how the eye and the brain contribute to illusion.

Books

For Teachers and Parents

Block, J. Richard, and Yuker, Harold E. *Can You Believe Your Eyes?* Gardner Press, Inc., 1989.

M.C. Escher: Twenty-nine Master Prints. Photos by William Wegman. Abrams Inc., 1983.

McKim, Robert H. *Experiences in Visual Thinking.* Prindle, Weber, & Schmidt, 1980.

Seymour, Dale, and Britton, Jill. *Introduction to Tessellations.* Dale Seymour Publications, 1989.

Simon, Seymour. *The Optical Illusion Book.* Beech Tree Books, 1976.

For Students

Brandreth, Gyles. *The Great Book of Optical Illusions.* Sterling Publishing Co., Inc., 1985.

Crystal, Nancy, and Tytla, Milan. *You Won't Believe Your Eyes.* Annick Press Ltd., 1992.

Jonas, Ann. *Reflections.* Greenwillow Books, 1987.

———. *Round Trip.* Greenwillow Books, 1983.

Lobel, Arnold. *The Turnaround Wind.* Harper & Row, 1988.

Magic Eye: A New Way of Looking at the World; 3D illusions by N. E. Thing Enterprises. Andrews and McMeel, 1993.

Simon, Seymour. *The Optical Illusion Book.* Beech Tree Books, 1976.

Answers to the worksheet: 1. They are the same. 2. They are the same. 3. They are the same. 4. All of the long lines are parallel. 5. The line segments are the same. 6. The angles are the same. 7. All of the shapes are perfect squares.

Geometrical Illusions

1. Which is larger, circle A or circle B?

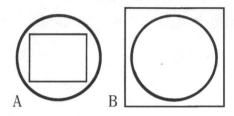

2. Which is larger, circle A or circle B?

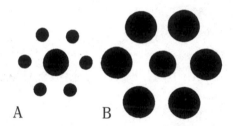

3. Which is larger, circle A or circle B?

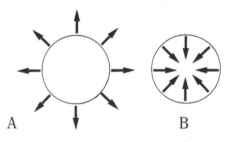

4. Are any of the long lines parallel? If so, which ones?

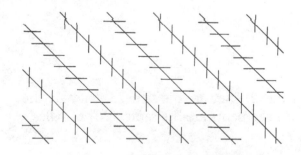

5. Which line segment is the longest?

6. Which inner angle is larger?

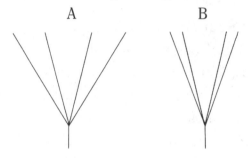

7. Are any of the shapes perfect squares? If so, which ones?

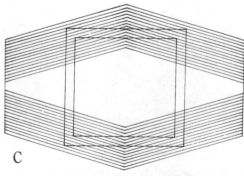

5: Adapted from CAN YOU BELIEVE YOUR EYES? by J. R. Block and Harold E. Yuker. Reprinted by permission of Y & B Associates, Hempstead, NY.
1, 2, 3, 4, 6, 7: From CAN YOU BELIEVE YOUR EYES? by J. R. Block and Harold E. Yuker. Reprinted by permission of Y & B Associates, Hempstead, NY.

Zoetrope

Inventing Moving Pictures

Using the Zoetrope to Show Movement

Inventors seldom develop their ideas in isolation. Frequently they build their work from the discoveries of many. This lesson contains ideas for a unit on inventions, including a look at the marvel of moving pictures. Creating flip cards and a zoetrope help explain this concept.

A Little History

One of the inventions that contributed to the development of film making was the zoetrope. This optical toy was created by W. Horner in 1834. The "Wheel of Life," as it was referred to, provided hours of entertainment. Figures, simply drawn on a strip of paper, were shown in progressive stages of action. Peering through slits in a spinning drum gave the sensation of motion and allowed the figures to spring to life.

Zoetrope

When we see the zoetrope in operation, the strip of several spinning, still images appear as one moving subject. By the time our brain receives one image, another is appearing. This delayed perception blends all the images together, giving the illusion of movement. Another example of this idea can be illustrated in a dark room with a full length mirror and a flashlight. Stand in front of the mirror and quickly whirl the flashlight round and round. A steady circle of light will be visible.

Materials

- 12" x 18" construction paper
- pencils
- rulers
- tape
- scissors
- colored pens
- adding machine tape (standard size–2 1/4")
- turntable, record player, or lazy Susan

Procedure

STEP 1.

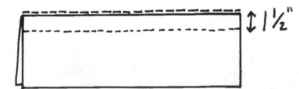

Fold a sheet of 12" x 18" construction paper in half lengthwise. Measure 1 1/2" down from the fold. With a pencil, draw a line parallel to the fold.

STEP 2.

Across the edge of the fold and directly below on the pencil line, measure and mark 1 1/2", then 1/4". Continue to mark these intervals

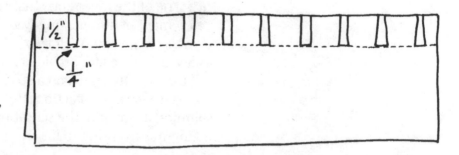

across the construction paper. Note: the measurement does not come out even. There is a 1/4" segment left over.

STEP 3.

With a ruler and pencil, draw a line connecting the marks on the fold with those on the pencil line. Cut along these lines from the fold to the pencil line, then cut out all the 1/4" segments.

STEP 4.

Hold the construction paper with the slits pointing up. Bring the two ends around to form the barrel shape of the zoetrope. Tape the ends in place so that it can stand by itself.

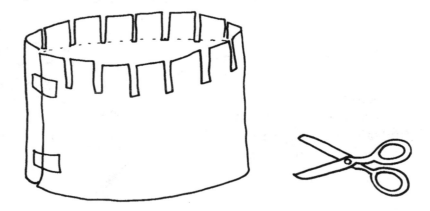

STEP 5.

Make the action frames to use in the zoetrope with a piece of adding machine tape about 17" long. With pencil and ruler divide the tape into a series of 1 1/2" frames.

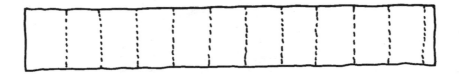

STEP 6.

Think about the different stages of an object or person in motion and decide how to represent this in a simple drawing.

STEP 7.

Plan the drawing, putting the different stages of the action sequentially in the frames. Draw first in pencil, avoiding details. Next, go back over the pencil lines with dark or bold colored pens.

STEP 8.

Finally bring the ends of the adding machine tape together to form a circle with the pictures on the inside. Overlap one end 1/2" and tape it in position on the outside of the circle.

STEP 9.

Place the zoetrope in the center of a turntable. Put the action strip inside the zoetrope resting on the bottom. Now spin the turntable and watch the drawings jump into action.

Flip Card

his quick and easy activity also creates the illusion of motion.

Materials

- 3" x 3" tagboard or white construction paper
- rubber bands (approx. 3" or longer)
- scissors
- pencil
- marking pens

Procedure

S T E P 1 .

One piece of 3" x 3" tagboard and a rubber band is needed for each flip card.

S T E P 2 .

Before experimenting with original ideas, draw the first flip card similar to the following illustration. On one side, draw a fish bowl with a dark color pen. Make the picture almost as large as the card. Turn the card over, hold it up to a window with the fishbowl upside down, and draw a fish so that it fits within the outline of the bowl. Color the fish with a bright color.

S T E P 3 .

Cut the rubber band into two equal pieces. At the center of each side edge (about 1/4" in), staple one end of the rubber band segment.

S T E P 4 .

Hold the end of each rubber band and spin the flip card back and forth between the thumb and forefinger. This creates the illusion that the fish is inside the bowl.

S T E P 5 .

Allow time for students to invent their own flip cards.

From *Art Connections*, published by GoodYearBooks. Copyright © 1995 Kimberly Boehler Thompson and Diana Standing Loftus.

Integrating Ideas

 here are many fascinating inventions associated with the history of filmmaking. While doing a unit on inventions consider the following:

- Discuss this quote by Albert Einstein: "Imagination is more important than knowledge." Who was Albert Einstein? Why did he say this? Do you agree? Why or why not?

- Read biographies of famous inventors. As a class, develop a list of characteristics they seem to have in common.

- Look in the dictionary for the origins of everyday words. Invent new words.

- Make a timeline showing inventions of a certain time period.

- Debate the advantages and disadvantages of the following: telephone, television, automobile, and the computer. How have inventions affected and changed our lives?

Books

For Teachers and Parents

Blond, Geri, and Spivack, Doris. *Inventions and Extensions*. Incentive Publications, Inc., 1991.

McCormack, Alan J. *Inventors Workshop*. Fearon Teacher Aids. Belmont, CA, 1981.

Robinson, David. *The History of World Cinema*. Stein and Day Publishers, 1973.

For Students

Bailey, Joseph H. *Small Inventions That Make a Big Difference*. Books for World Explorers. National Geographic Society, 1984.

Caney, Steven. *Steven Caney's Invention Handbook*. Workman Publishing Co., 1985.

Davidson, Margaret. *Louis Braille*. Scholastic Inc., 1971.

Gibbons, Gail. *Lights, Camera, Action*. Harper, 1989.

Jenkins, Patrick. *Animation*. Addison-Wesley Publishing Co., Inc., 1991.

Jones, Charlotte Folt. *Mistakes That Worked*. Doubleday, 1991.

Latham, Jean Lee. *Eli Whitney*. Chelsea Juniors, 1991.

Lepscky, Ibi. *Albert Einstein*. Barron's, 1982.

Walpole, Brenda. *Fun with Science*. Warwick Press, 1987.

From *Art Connections*, published by GoodYearBooks. Copyright © 1995 Kimberly Boehler Thompson and Diana Standing Loftus.

Architecture

The Facade of Economics

> "Architecture is frozen music."
>
> *Johann Wolfgang von Goethe, German writer, 1749–1832*

Becoming Planners and Designers of Architecture

Experiences that emulate the real world within the classroom are important. In this lesson, students explore various roles as planners, designers, and construction workers. They calculate the cost of materials for their project and submit their ideas to a classroom planning committee.

A Little History

The Parthenon, a Greek Temple built in 447 B.C., has stood the test of time. Although the walls of this masterpiece may be crumbling, the design lives on. Those Greek designs, considered by some to be proportionally perfect, have influenced nearly every Western culture from Ancient Rome to Modern Europe and the United States.

From *Art Connections*, published by GoodYearBooks. Copyright © 1995 Kimberly Boehler Thompson and Diana Standing Loftus.

Some of our state capitol buildings, including the U.S. Mint in Philadelphia and the Treasury Building in Washington, D.C., reflect the ideas of the early Greeks. However, the architecture found in the United States can best be described in much the same manner as its people–a melting pot. U.S. architectural influences range from Native Americans to people from the most far-reaching continents. A visit to New Orleans would reveal traces of French architecture. In our oldest city, St. Augustine, Florida, we'd find Spanish architecture; while in Sitka, Alaska, one would see a Russian influence. Africans can be credited for developing the veranda, which is most commonly found in the South. Adobe can be attributed to the Southwestern Native Americans.

Project

Architectural Mural

Students construct a street scene of building facades to attach to a wall of the classroom, hallway, lunchroom, or stage. The experience is an opportunity to learn about architectural elements, building guidelines, and scale measurement.

Materials

- posterboard
- cardboard
- construction paper
- pencil
- ruler
- drawing paper
- colored pens
- scissors
- tape
- paste
- glue

Procedure

STEP 1.

Students can work independently or in groups to plan their designs. Determine a scale for everyone to use. For example, the construction scale for the mural can be 1" to 1'. (An 8-inch door would then equal 8 feet.) To draw this to scale, let 1/4" equal 1'. Students should decide on the finished dimensions of their building and draw it to scale.

STEP 2.

When drawings are complete, have students submit their plans to a classroom planning committee. This committee decides on code requirements of size, taking into consideration standard sizes of posterboard or other available materials. They can also decide if the buildings in the mural are going to be zoned residential or commercial.

STEP 3.

Another classroom committee can determine costs for the materials that will be used. Posterboard and other sheet materials can be priced by the square inch. Paper strips or decorative tape can be priced by the linear inch. Have the rest of the students estimate their construction costs and plan for the most efficient use of their materials.

STEP 4.

Begin construction by making the basic size and shape of the facade out of posterboard. Then plan the sequence for adding other elements such as the roof, siding, chimney, porch, door, stairs, columns, and windows.

Be imaginative with building materials. Consider construction paper, corrugated cardboard, contact paper, foil, gift wrap, wallpaper, fabric, wood scraps, and found objects. Be inventive with the remaining details: siding materials (boards, brick, or stone), shingles for the roof, door and window frames, trim, doors that open and close, door knobs, a porch light, window shutters, curtains, or planter boxes. Interior scenes can be cut from magazines and pasted in windows or behind doors.

STEP 5.

When the class has finished all construction, decide on the mural arrangement and fasten against the chosen wall with masking tape.

Integrating Ideas

o extend the previous ideas mentioned, consider the following:

⊚ Make copies of the reproducible pages. Discuss architectural features and descriptions with the class. Search through magazines for examples of the features. Paste and label them into a book or a collage. There are several helpful books which describe origins of style. Two outstanding introductions to the subject are *What Style Is It?* published by the National Trust for Historic Preservation, Washington, D.C., and *Clues to American Architecture* written by Marilyn Klein and David Fogle.

⊚ Take a walk around the neighborhood or visit a nearby business district with interesting architecture. Pay particular attention to the faces of the buildings. Are the designs symmetrical or asymmetrical? Try to identify different structural features, building materials, and the historical influence of the styles.

⊚ Arrange to have the class visit with a city planner. Ask questions about building codes and energy requirements. Find out about preservation programs, the program's guidelines, and why the guidelines are important.

⊚ Make an architectural mural with a unit on Colonial History or Native Americans.

Books

For Teachers and Parents

Upton, Dell, ed. *America's Architectural Roots.* The Preservation Press, 1986.

D'Alelio, Jane. *I Know That Building! Discovering Architecture with Activities and Games.* The Preservation Press, 1989.

Klein, Marilyn W., and Fogle, David P. *Clues to American Architecture.* Starrhill Press, 1985.

Mueller, Mary Korstad. *Murals: Creating an Environment.* Davis Publications, Inc., 1979.

Poppeliers, John; Chambers, S. Allen; and Schwartz, Nancy B. *What Style Is It?* The Preservation Press, 1984.

For Students

Bare, Colleen Stanley. *This Is a House.* Cobblehill Books. Dutton, 1992.

Eisen, David. *Fun with Architecture.* The Metropolitan Museum of Art. Viking, 1992.

Goodall, John S. *Great Days of a Country House.* MacMillan Publishing Co., 1992.

Isaacson, Phillip. *Round Buildings, Square Buildings, Buildings That Wiggle Like a Fish.* Knopf, 1990.

James, Alan. *Castles and Mansions.* Lerner Publishing Co., 1989.

Macaulay, David. *Castle.* Houghton Mifflin Co., 1977.

———. *Cathedral: The Story of Its Construction.* Houghton Mifflin, 1973.

Architects Make Zig Zags: Looking at Architecture from A-Z; illus. by Roxie Munro. Preservation Press, 1986.

Von Tscharner, Renata and Fleming, Ronald Lee. *New Providence: A Changing Cityscape.* The Preservation Press, 1992.

Wilson, Forrest. *What It Feels Like to Be a Building.* The Preservation Press, 1988.

There are unlimited terms to describe architectural features. Learning a few basic characteristics will set a foundation for expanding this vocabulary and develop an awareness of style. The following reproducible pages can be used by students as a guide for describing and identifying common building features. Have them cut examples from magazines, or sketch their own examples.

Architectural Features

Facade–The face or front of a building

Symmetrical–Both sides of the facade are the same; the design is exactly balanced

Asymmetrical–The size, shape, or position of elements on the two sides of the facade will vary

Roof Terms

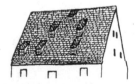

Pitch–The angle or slant of the roof

Eaves–The projecting lower edge of the roof

Gambrel–Ridged roof with two slopes on each side; the lower slope will have the steepest pitch

Hip roof–Has four equally pitched sides

Gambrel: From glossary by Matthew J. Mosca from WHAT STYLE IS IT? by John C. Poppeliers, S. Allen Chambers, Jr., and Nancy B. Schwartz. Copyright © 1983 National Trust for Historic Preservation in the United States. Reprinted by permission of The Preservation Press.
All others: From CLUES TO AMERICAN ARCHITECTURE by Marilyn W. Klein and David P. Fogle. Illustrated by Wolcott B. Etienne. Copyright © 1985, 1986 by Wolcott B. Etienne. Illustrations © 1985, 1986 by Marilyn W. Klein and David P. Fogle. Reprinted by permission of Starrhill Press.

Shed or lean-to–A roof with only one slope

Mansard–A roof with two slopes on all four sides

Gable roof–Double-sloping roof that forms a triangular wall section at each end; the triangular section is called the gable

Window Types

Dormer–Window that projects from a sloping roof; also the roof structure holding the window

Palladian Window–Classic style window with an arched central section and a rectangular section on each side

Bay Window–Window projecting out from the wall

Fanlight–Semicircular window, the shape of a fan, with radiating bars, placed over a door or window

Porches and Entrances

Pediment–A wide, low-pitched, classical style gable on the facade of a building; also a triangular crown over doors and windows

Porch–The covered entrance to a building; it usually has a separate roof and can be enclosed

Gallery–Outdoor balcony or corridor; in the south, a porch or veranda

Veranda–A roofed, open porch attached to the exterior of a building

Portico–A major porch; it often has a pedimented roof supported by columns

Decorative Elements

Spindle–A turned wooden element used for stair railing and porch trim

Balustrade–A series of vase-shaped posts (balusters) supporting a rail

Battlement–A parapet with open spaces for defense or decoration

Parapet–Low protective wall or railing around the edge of a roof or balcony

Turret–Small tower at the corner of a building, often containing a staircase

Column

A supporting pillar, usually with a round shaft, capital, and base.

Doric–The oldest and simplest of Greek columns; fluted, with no base and saucer-shaped capitals

Ionic–Classical Greek style rec gnized by the capital with two opposed volutes (scroll-like ornaments)

Corinthian–The most elaborate columns from Classical Greek architecture, with a slender fluted shaft and decorated bell-shaped capital

Pilaster–A shallow pier attached to a wall and decorated to resemble a column

Bibliography

Anderson, Charles R. *Lettering.* Van Nostrand Reinhold Company, l982.

Appleton, Le Roy H. *American Indian Design and Decoration.* Dover Publications, Inc., 1971.

Baratta-Lorton. *Mathematics: A Way of Thinking.* Addison Publishing Company, 1977.

Beeler, Nelson F. and Branley, Franklyn M. *Experiments in Optical Illusion.* Thomas Y. Crowell Co., 1951.

Brooks, Mona. *Drawing with Children.* Jeremy P. Tarcher, Inc., 1986.

Burns, Marilyn. *About Teaching Mathematics: A K–8 Resource.* Marilyn Burns Education Associates, 1992.

California State Board of Education. *Visual and Performing Arts Framework for California Public Schools: Kindergarten Through Grade 12,* rev. ed. California State Publications, 1989.

Caine, Renate Nummela and Caine, Geoffrey. *Making Connections: Teaching and the Human Brain.* Association for Supervision and Curriculum Development, 1991.

Cheatham, Frank; Cheatham, Jane; and Haler, Sheryl. *Design Concepts and Applications.* Prentice-Hall, Inc., 1983.

Cole, Bruce and Gealt, Adelheid. *Art of the Western World.* Simon & Schuster, 1989.

Dissanayake, Ellen. *What Is Art For?* University of Washington Press, 1988.

Edwards, Betty. *Drawing on the Right Side of the Brain.* Jeremy P. Tarcher, Inc., rev. ed. 1989.

Ellinger, Richard G. *Color, Structure, and Design.* Van Nostrand Reinhold Company, 1980.

Encyclopedia Americana. Grolier Incorporated, vol. 1 and 27. 1990.

Evers, Inge. *Feltmaking: Techniques and Projects.* Lark Books, 1987.

Feetham, Ann. "Thomas Jefferson, Architect." *Cobblestone Magazine,* vol. 9 (August 1988), pp. 11–13.

Feldman, Edmund Burke. *Becoming Human Through Art: Aesthetic Experience in the School.* Prentice-Hall, Inc., 1970.

Foote, Timothy. "A Tale of Some Tails and the Story of Their Sky Creator." *Smithsonian Magazine,* vol. 19, no. 10 (1989).

Finn, David. *How to Visit a Museum.* Harry N. Abrams, Inc., 1985.

Fleming, William. *Arts & Ideas.* Holt, Rinehart and Winston, Inc., 1986.

Fowler, Virginia. *Paperworks.* Prentice Hall, Inc., 1982.

Gardner, Helen. *Art Through the Ages;* revised by Horst De La Croix and Richard Tansey. Harcourt Brace Jovanovich, Inc., 1975.

Gregory, R. L. and Gombrich, E. H. *Illusion in Nature and Art.* Charles Scribner's Sons, 1973.

Harman, Willis. *Global Mind Change.* Knowledge Systems, Inc., 1988.

Hart, Michael H. *The 100: A Ranking of the Most Influential Persons in History.* Hart Publishing Co., 1978.

Heller, Jules. *Papermaking.* Watson-Guptill Publications, 1978.

———. *Printmaking Today.* Holt, Rinehart and Winston, Inc., 1972.

Hoffberg, Judith. *Paper–Art and Technology.* Artists' Books, 1981.

Klein, Marilyn W. and Fogle, David P. *Clues to American Architecture.* Starrhill Press, 1985.

Lanners, Edi. *Illusions.* Holt, Rinehart and Winston, 1977.

McKim, Robert H. *Experiences in Visual Thinking.* Prindle, Weber & Schmidt, 1980.

Meglin, Nick. *The Art of Humorous Illustration.* Watson-Guptill Publications, 1981.

National Endowment for the Arts. *Toward Civilization: A Report On Arts Education.* U.S. Government Printing Office, 1988.

Oregon Department Of Education. *Art Education Common Curriculum Goals.* Publications and Multimedia Center, 1990.

Oregon State University. *Lesson Plan Units for Forestry Education.* Oregon State University, 1982.

Pine, Tillie and Levine, Joseph. *The Chinese Knew.* McGraw-Hill Book Company Inc., 1958.

Poppeliers, John; Chambers, S. Allen, Jr.; and Schwartz, Nancy B. *What Style Is It?* The Preservation Press, 1981.

Porter, Tom, and Goodman, Sue. *Manual of Graphic Techniques 2: For Architects, Graphic Designers, & Artists.* Charles Scribner's Sons, 1982.

Robertson, Bruce. *Lettering Workbooks: Designing with Letters.* Watson-Guptill Publications, 1989.

Robinson, David. *The History of World Cinema.* Stein and Day Publishers, 1973.

Shahn, Ben. *The Shape of Content.* Harvard University Press, 1978.

Shoemaker, Betty. "Integrative Education: A Curriculum for the Twenty-First Century." vol. 33, no. 2. Oregon School Study Council. University of Oregon, 1989.

Sullivan, George. *Understanding Architecture.* Frederick Warne & Co., Inc., 1971.

Texas Education Agency. *Art Education: Planning for Teaching and Learning.* Publications Distributions Office. Austin, Texas. 1988.

Upton, Dell. *American Architectural Roots.* The Preservation Press, 1986.

Wescher, Herta. *Wolf Collage.* Harry N. Abrams, Inc., 1968.

Wadsworth, Virginia Evarts. "Julia Morgan: America's Best Known Woman Architect." *Cobblestone Magazine,* vol. 9. (1988).

World Book Encyclopedia. World Book, Inc. Volume 19. 1989.